the technology director's guide to leadership

the power of great questions

Don Hall

International Society for Technology in Education
EUGENE, OREGON • WASHINGTON, DC

The Technology Director's Guide to Leadership
The Power of Great Questions
Don Hall

Director of Book Publishing: *Courtney Burkholder*
Acquisitions Editor: *Jeff V. Bolkan*
Production Editors: *Lanier Brandau and Lynda Gansel*
Production Coordinator: *Rachel Bannister*
Graphic Designer and Cover Design: *Signe Landin*
Rights and Permissions Administrator: *Lanier Brandau*
Copy Editor: *Katherine Clayton*
Indexer: *Ken Hassman*
Book Design and Production: *Kim McGovern*

Library of Congress Cataloging-in-Publication Data

Hall, Don (Donald Robert), 1962-
    The technology director's guide to leadership : the power of great questions / Don Hall. — 1st ed.
        p. cm.
    Includes bibliographical references and index.
    ISBN 978-1-56484-244-2 (pbk.)
        1. College personnel management. 2. Leadership. 3. Educational technology—Management.   I. International Society for Technology in Education. II. Title.
    LB2331.66.H35 2008
    378.1'1—dc22

                                                                                        2008028569

First Edition
ISBN: 978-1-56484-244-2

Printed in the United States of America

International Society for Technology in Education (ISTE)
Washington, DC, Office:
        1710 Rhode Island Ave. NW, Suite 900, Washington, DC 20036-3132
Eugene, Oregon, Office:
        180 West 8th Ave., Ste 300, Eugene, OR 97401-2916
Order Desk: 1.800.336.5191
Order Fax: 1.541.302.3778
Customer Service: orders@iste.org
Book Publishing: books@iste.org
Rights and Permissions: permissions@iste.org
Web: www.iste.org

About ISTE

The International Society for Technology in Education (ISTE) is the trusted source for professional development, knowledge generation, advocacy, and leadership for innovation. A nonprofit membership association, ISTE provides leadership and service to improve teaching, learning, and school leadership by advancing the effective use of technology in PK–12 and teacher education.

Home of the National Educational Technology Standards (NETS), the Center for Applied Research in Educational Technology (CARET), and the National Educational Computing Conference (NECC), ISTE represents more than 85,000 professionals worldwide. We support our members with information, networking opportunities, and guidance as they face the challenge of transforming education. To find out more about these and other ISTE initiatives, visit our website at **www.iste.org**.

As part of our mission, ISTE Book Publishing works with experienced educators to develop and produce practical resources for classroom teachers, teacher educators, and technology leaders. Every manuscript we select for publication is carefully peer-reviewed and professionally edited. We look for content that emphasizes the effective use of technology where it can make a difference—increasing the productivity of teachers and administrators; helping students with unique learning styles, abilities, or backgrounds; collecting and using data for decision making at the school and district levels; and creating dynamic, project-based learning environments that engage 21st-century learners. We value your feedback on this book and other ISTE products. E-mail us at **books@iste.org**.

About the Author

 As a career educator with more than 20 years' experience in teaching and administration at the K–12 and university levels, **Don Hall** has held senior leadership roles with the General Electric (GE) Corporation and the Kentucky Department of Education. Don is a veteran conference presenter at the national and international levels, published author, and experienced consultant. In 2007, Don Hall accepted the position of Chief Information Officer with the 34,000-student Muscogee County Public Schools in Columbus, GA.

Previously, Don spent seven years as CIO for Information Technology with the 27,000 student Kent School District in the Seattle metropolitan area, which is known nationally for its use of technology to improve instruction. Under his leadership, the district was recognized as a Microsoft National Center of Excellence for achievements in this area. He has also served in similar roles in Tennessee and Kentucky.

Don serves as a columnist with the International Society for Technology in Education (ISTE) magazine, *Learning & Leading with Technology.* In addition he has served on numerous national educational advisory boards, including COSN, ISTE, HP, and Microsoft.

In recognition of his contributions to public education, he was presented the 2006 *Educational Technology Leader of the Year* award by the *Technology & Learning* journal and was runner-up for the 2006 *National Public School CIO of the Year* award.

Don says, "Growing up as the oldest of three children in a single parent family in an impoverished area of rural eastern Kentucky, I experienced first-hand the inequities that exist in society. However, education provided me the means to improve the quality of life for my family and myself. As a result, I have committed my time and energies to serving students and their families by helping them discover the joys of learning and capitalize on the promise that technology offers for extending learning into exciting new dimensions."

Acknowledgments

I want to thank Dr. Barbara Grohe, Superintendent of the Kent School District, and the late Dr. Roy L. Ragsdale, for whom I had the privilege of working in two different districts. They were instrumental in shaping my professional growth and allowing me to develop, test, and refine many of the techniques and models contained in the book. They also served as good role models for what effective leadership can look like in public education.

Dedication

In order to achieve your goals, it takes people who support and believe in you from the very beginning up to the point the goal is realized. As the often quoted African proverb says, "It takes a village to raise a child." I believe that I am a product of one of those villages.

- For me that began with my grandmother, Nellie G. Lewis, who never got beyond the second grade but was one of the smartest and wisest women I ever knew. She was also the first person to tell me that I was special and was meant to do great things.

- Next in the line came my elementary lunch lady, Bernice Stafford, who always made sure I had a warm smile each day as I came through the lunch line and extra food, because she knew that I might not go home to enough that night. She showed me that every person in the district can make a difference in a student's life.

- Then came my high school math teacher, Ms. Edna Mae Love, who was the hardest teacher I ever had and did not cut me any slack because I was poor or bright. However, she did sacrifice her lunch break to teach me calculus because our school did not offer it. She demonstrated that you must have high standards for all students, but you must care about them as people first.

- Next was our community public librarian who drove the bookmobile, Helen Rayburn. She made sure I had enough books to satisfy my insatiable love of reading, which was especially difficult because I read so many and books were a scarce resource in my home. She opened the doors to my love of reading and learning.

- Finally, my beautiful wife Debbie and wonderful daughter Sarah who love me unconditionally and have taught me what that means. They opened my heart to a depth of caring that I did not know was possible, which has changed me as a leader. My wife has supported me throughout my career unflinchingly as we moved across the country and has been my biggest cheerleader. My daughter serves as a living symbol of why I stay in this fight to make a difference in public education.

Contents

Preface

In this book, I use three characters to exhibit leadership styles, the sage, sensei, and oracle. You may wonder where I derived the inspiration for the sage, sensei, and oracle. Actually, it is not from any single source. It grew out of an amalgamation of ideas gleaned from years of reading mythology, comic books, and classical literature. As I read through the different genres, I often saw similar patterns appear in how character types were portrayed. So when I began trying to build a leadership model, those three roles seemed like a natural way to divide the continuum of behaviors that I have observed in leaders. I also thought they would be easy for people to identify with because they were so commonly used in popular media and literature.

chapter 1

a modern
leadership fable

The names in this fable have been changed to protect the innocent—namely, you and me. After all, most of us will find a bit of ourselves in all the characters featured in this exploration of the difficult journey toward becoming an effective technology leader.

Max's Journey

Max Seeker looked down at his watch, anxiously realizing that the meeting was running long. He listened to the discussion ramble on about possible solutions to address yet another challenge in a series of missteps in his team's deployment of the wireless network. Just a few weeks ago, Max had thought the project was going well. Then the team ran into a fairly significant snag in a couple of the older buildings, and things just seemed to spin out of control. Now they were in constant firefighting mode.

Max had called his senior technical staff together to try to identify possible fixes for the latest problem. He knew that if they did not remedy the situation in a timely manner, all of the positive buzz they had generated with the project would be lost. As he listened to his team, he grew increasingly frustrated at their inability to develop a practical strategy. He finally stood up and said, "OK, I need to bring this meeting to a close. I have some other important meetings to attend off-site. I'll count on you all to continue working together to develop a proposal to present to me first thing tomorrow morning. Remember, we have to solve this problem as soon as possible."

With this statement, Max walked out the door, leaving the group mumbling and grumbling.

Max knew the predicament was not really his team's fault. The department had rushed to get the project done. They had not been able to plan adequately, and the project was not funded properly. However, the board told him that it had to be implemented by the opening of the school year. The pressure was in response to an adjacent school district's successful launch of a wireless network, a project that had received a lot of positive press coverage. Max was amazed by what could drive the decision-making process.

As Max began driving to the local university, he replayed the events of the last year in his mind. It had been a tumultuous time, to say the least. He could still hear his supervisor's flattering words: "Max, I've got a great opportunity for you. I want you to assume the leadership of the technology program. I know you'll do a great job."

Eagerly—and probably a bit naively—Max jumped at the chance to take the leadership reins. He loved working with technology and knew he could make a positive difference in the lives of students. The job had seemed like a perfect fit.

Wow, what a difference a year can make, he thought.

During the past few months, Max had been through the blender. His schedule had been full of many projects competing for his time: struggling with the demands of ensuring the wireless network was implemented; getting the data warehouse online so the schools could figure out how to conduct their Adequate Yearly Progress (AYP) analysis for the No Child Left Behind act (NCLB); modifying the student information system so parents could securely access data over the Internet; and managing high employee turnover and competition from the private sector.

Max was at his limit. The worst part was that he felt like he was not really providing effective leadership for his staff. Out of desperation, he signed up for leadership training at the local university. He had set aside time today to meet with the three professors who would be teaching the classes during the upcoming term. Max enjoyed learning new things; it energized him. He felt a sense of accomplishment when he shared new knowledge with others.

Max arrived at the campus and parked in the first available spot. As he approached the graduate school building, he felt the weight of the past few months pressing down on him. His breathing was labored, and his chest was tight. As he walked down the hallway looking for the specified office, he hoped very much that his professors could provide some answers.

Approaching the first office on the left, Max noticed a name lettered neatly on the dark oak door in large, elegant letters: Professor B. A. Sage. He knocked softly on the door, and a deep, resonant voice answered, "Come in." Max scanned the office and noticed that it was decorated with great attention to every detail. It was neat, organized, and exuded an air of authority. The walls were covered with numerous degrees and certificates denoting expertise in a variety of areas.

Professor Sage peered up at Max over a pair of gold-rimmed glasses. Dignified and fastidiously dressed, he fit into the environment perfectly.

"I assume you must be Mr. Seeker," Professor Sage intoned.

"Yes, sir. I came here seeking guidance. I'm an administrator in a local school district and was planning to take leadership training here this semester. I want to ask you a few simple questions, if I may?"

"But, of course," the professor replied.

Max, feeling a bit out of place in the tidy environment, asked tentatively, "What does it take to be an effective leader?"

"You have certainly come to the right person," said the professor, "You should feel very relieved that your journey led you to my door. This is clearly not an easy question, so I can see why you are perplexed, but fear not, I can give you the answers you seek. There are 32 different domains that make up effective leadership. Of course, all of these are comprehensively outlined in my latest book. First, though, I suggest you begin by taking copious notes of what I am about to tell you. Then, you will need to study my treatise on effective leadership strategies, so you'll be prepared to benefit from the next set of activities I have in mind for you."

Overwhelmed, Max's eyes started to glaze over. He wasn't sure this professor's style was going to work for him. He let the professor speak for a bit and then remembered his next appointment. Glancing at his watch, he said, "I am so sorry, but I need to go now. Maybe we can pick up where we left off at another time."

Professor Sage said, "Yes, yes, go if you must. Good luck, and I will anticipate your prompt return, because we have so much more to cover." The professor returned to his reading, muttering, "That young man is clearly not ready to learn or to lead. That's too bad—there is so much I could teach him."

Max continued down the hallway, thinking, *Wow, that guy was full of himself.* Max found the next office he needed to visit. Once again there was lettering on the door, stenciled in silver and green reflective letters: Professor Ima Oracle.

As Max opened the door, the first thing he encountered was a thick, purple cloud. He started coughing.

"Oh dear, oh dear," said a melodic voice from within the cloud, "I am so sorry." Max heard a fan click on, and the room began to clear. He almost let out a chuckle as he saw the office. Talk about a contrast from Professor Sage's environment.

Professor Oracle's room was an eclectic mix of 1960s hippy, modern earth-mother, and other random and hard-to-classify styles. Many plants lined the window ledges and bookcases while most of her books sat in stacks on the floor. A fountain bubbled in the corner.

Standing in the middle of it all was a tall woman dressed in a floor-length, natural-fiber skirt. She wore a turban, sandals, and numerous bracelets that jingled and clanked as she motioned him into the office. Her expression was warm and contented, and her face was etched with lines of life experience.

"Excuse me, Professor Oracle. I'm Max Seeker. We have an appointment."

"Oh, we do? Oh, yes, we do. It's a pleasure to meet you. I'm so glad that you came," she replied. She turned, rummaging through piles of papers on her desk, looking for what he assumed was her schedule. "Yes, I remember now. Please sit down," she said as she scooped up a pile of books from a chair, depositing them on another chair. She motioned for him to sit down. "What can I help you with?"

"Well, I am an administrator with a local school district, and I plan to take leadership classes here next semester," Max explained.

"Yes, I strongly concur with that course of action," Professor Oracle replied, starting to rise as if the meeting were over.

"No, no, that was not my question," Max interjected.

"Oh, you have another question?" The professor gazed at him expectantly.

"Yes. I am wondering what you think it takes to be an effective leader."

"That is a very good question, Max. I suggest you research it. There are lots of good books on the topic and many good teachers as well. There are good teachers here at this university, and I can introduce you to them. Everyone's opinion is valuable. I also believe that much of what it takes to be a good leader is within you already. What do you think?"

Without waiting for a response, Professor Oracle said, "Well, Max, I hope that helps you, as I really do enjoy helping students. However, now I must prepare for my next seminar, 'The Nature and Nurture of Teams.'" Professor Oracle stood up and began gathering a bundle of multicolored scarves.

Max stood in stunned silence for a second, and then said, "Well, thank you, Professor, I guess." He turned and left her office, not sure what to make of what had just happened. "Well, that's not quite what I expected, to say the least. I don't know if I got an answer or just more questions."

As he approached the last door on the right, he noticed the simple lettering on it: Noah Sensei. Max hesitantly knocked. The door opened, and in the entrance appeared an average-looking gentleman with a broad smile across his face and his hand outstretched. "Please come in, Max."

As Max looked around the office, he almost felt at home. It reminded Max of his own office. It was a place where work occurred—not too neat but not too messy. There were stacks of student papers and projects, but he saw they were mostly organized in folders. Yet it was obvious Professor Sensei was working on them. The bookshelves were lined with lots of books—many of which had creased spines, showing they had been used frequently. The office had a small table with six chairs around it, and a white board with notes on it. Evidently, the professor conducted small-group conferences in here as well. Max was impressed.

Professor Sensei set down the book he was carrying and motioned for Max to sit down. "Now, Max, how may I help you today?"

Max recounted his work situation as he had done with the other two professors. With a bit of exasperation, he described his two previous meetings. The professor merely listened, nodding occasionally. Finally, he said, "I think I understand why you're here. But first I must ask, what leads you to think you can dismiss Professor Sage and Professor Oracle so easily?"

The question took Max by surprise, especially because he thought he and Professor Sensei had a lot in common. Frustrated, he said, "Well, it seems they really don't have a clue about leadership. Professor Sage is a pompous, self-important lecturer, and Professor Oracle seems pretty scattered and disorganized."

"When one is a true seeker, he realizes that everyone teaches him something and that all lessons are a valuable gift to be honored," Professor Sensei tersely responded.

A moment of uncomfortable silence passed between the two of them. Glancing around, Max noticed the author of the book Professor Sensei had been carrying was B. A. Sage.

Professor Sensei said, "What you do not realize, Max, is that Professor Sage came to the university as an expert in large-scale project management, having been responsible for deploying information technology systems for the military. And Professor Oracle was a senior VP for an international company and designed its Center for Educational Leadership and Training Program, which has now become a model for the private sector. So, although their leadership styles may be quite different from yours, clearly you can learn much from them."

Max sat quietly, pondering what he had heard.

The professor then queried, "So what did you specifically come to see *me* for today?"

Gathering his composure, Max asked for a third time, "What does it take to be an effective leader?"

Professor Sensei thought for a moment and then said, "Max, you have taken the first step. You have asked the question. Now come walk with me, and let's talk more about it."

What Max learned from his journey is that leadership styles can be quite different and questions can be quite powerful. Although the journey begins with a question, the real power lies in the dialogue that follows. I invite you to journey with Max as we learn more about powerful leadership questions and the ways they can help you become a more effective leader.

Individuals are often tapped for technology leadership roles because of their expertise in technology or instruction; however, they are seldom trained in how to be leaders and agents of change at the organizational level. Yet the one thing we are coming to realize is that technology leaders (Chief Information Officer [CIO], Chief Technology Officer [CTO], technology directors, and even many technology coordinators) are increasingly being called upon to assume the mantle of leadership.

Power Questions

- Why did you select this book?
- What knowledge and skills are you hoping to learn by reading this book?
- How are you like Max? How are you different?
- Do you see yourself in one of the professors? If so, which one?

chapter 2

what kind
of leader am I?

*I start with the premise
that the function of leadership
is to produce more leaders,
not more followers.*

Ralph Nader,
consumer advocate and politician

Congratulations! Just like Max, you have taken that all-important first step on your personal journey into improving your leadership abilities. Actually, you take steps along that journey of discovery every day. You have probably asked yourself the question, "What kind of leader am I?" This is a valuable question, one that has two very different questions buried within it.

The first question that probably comes to mind relates to the *quality* of leadership you provide. The second, less obvious question relates to the leadership *style* you use within your organization. In this chapter, we will explore both aspects.

Theory

Now that you have met our cast of players, you must be thinking, what do they have to do with being a good technology leader? These characters can help us delve into some of the painful leadership realities that we all face.

Understanding leadership is almost like asking, "What is the meaning of life?" We know that's a mammoth question, but we often try to find the answer in bite-sized wisdom. So we run around looking for easy answers by attending conferences, listening to leadership seminar tapes, attending college classes, and reading books and articles. But none of these seem to provide the quick fix we were seeking. Some of us take an alternate route: Having decided there are no easy answers, we decide not to ask the big questions.

Now, before you despair and toss this book into the fireplace, let me say it *is* possible to learn how to be a highly effective leader who can have a positive and powerful influence in your organization. It does take a lot of work and very specific skills and intentional strategies. Success is not usually achieved through accident or trial and error. True, you can learn lessons through those methods, but they are slow and costly. It's better to have a plan.

Let's begin by exploring the ideas behind the Leadership Continuum Model (LCM) to see what we can learn. In our fable, we saw three leadership archetypes: the *sage*, the *sensei*, and the *oracle*. These three leadership types make up the Leadership Continuum Model, illustrated in Figure 2.1. In the fable, the types were portrayed in the extreme to emphasize a particular aspect of the archetypes.

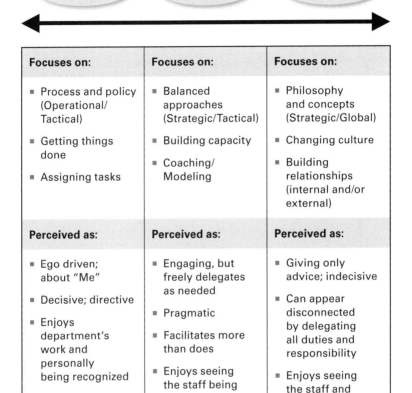

Figure 2.1. Leadership Continuum Model featuring the three leadership archetypes

It is important to note that each leadership type is neither negative nor positive within its own right. Each is merely different from the others. The LCM shows the *sage* and *oracle* as the extremes in the continuum with the *sensei* being the balance between the two.

The Sage

The *sage* represents the authoritarian type of leader whose motto might best be described as "I want you to do this specific task." Often they even prescribe the specific way the task is to be done. The sage usually sees a project's goals as more important than maintaining a sense of shared ownership or a positive climate. Sages want the right to provide input on nearly all decisions and often have final say on most of them. Although sages are directive, it is not necessarily because they are blind to the need for the involvement of others; it is more that they are driven by the need to ensure the success of the established goals. Sages have an intrinsically high degree of focus and often get frustrated when others do not exhibit this behavior. When working with direct reports, a sage may seek some input, or may not seek any at all. Sages generally give team members specific actions to perform.

Generally, sages will not delegate decision making for several reasons. They may believe their team members are not as competent as themselves. They may fear personal failure because they are accountable for the outcome. They may believe decision making is their main role as the leader. As a result of this high degree of ownership for decision making, they also believe they have earned the right for personal recognition for successes derived from the organization's efforts. This attitude can cause a great deal of frustration and low staff morale for team members who were critical to accomplishing the work. Sages are about control and personal recognition.

The Sensei

The *sensei* represents the dual role of mentor and facilitator. As the mentor, the focus is on assisting individuals with growth and problem solving, while the facilitator makes things happen by understanding the larger context of the project and the key components necessary to accomplish it effectively. In general, a sensei often takes longer to effect change initially, but the changes that occur are usually sustained.

The sensei has very high expectations for his or her team, from direct reports to lower-level positions. These expectations are driven by organizational values and goals. The mechanism for the sensei to reach both levels of team members is through extensive coaching and mentoring of those who work the closest with him or her. The focus is on building leadership capacity with the expectation that the knowledge and skills will be passed on throughout the rest of the team.

Because of this diffusion strategy focused on systemic change, a sensei can be viewed as someone who doesn't get the "quick wins." Instead, a sensei is looking to build practices and processes that are sustainable, which translates to a longer timeline of three to five years. This type of leader is trying to change culture and behaviors while implementing projects. A sensei is also trying to create a broader pool of leaders throughout his or her department.

This doesn't mean a sensei cannot execute projects effectively—that is where the focus on organizational goals comes into play. But a sensei will attempt to implement projects with an eye on whether the projects were executed according to the organization's values. Balance is important to this leadership archetype.

The Oracle

The *oracle* leadership style lives primarily in the world of global and abstract ideas. Oracles are most concerned with attitudes and relationships. They may choose to own decision making personally or delegate it to others. They also are concerned with ensuring that stakeholders understand projects and jargon in terms that are meaningful and relevant. Oracles are truly big-picture people; however, they sometimes cannot come down out of the clouds long enough to see the streets. An oracle's strength is seeing the organization or district's strategic goals. Oracles know how to recognize patterns and relationships, and they know the importance of relationships to accomplishing the work of the department or organization. It is through these connections that they move the work forward.

Some oracles build strong alliances with other departments so they can better understand the organization or district's needs and priorities. Other leaders of this type will delegate this responsibility to their staff. This second strategy is where oracles can fall into trouble. Oracles must not abdicate the role of relationship-building outside the department. When they do, they run the risk of appearing disconnected from the department and from the district or organization as a whole.

Oracles naturally delegate. They trust the relationships they form within their department. This is a two-edged sword. There is a limit to appropriate delegation. At one extreme, if you delegate too little, then you never build the capacity of your team, and you get buried in day-to-day tactical operations. In contrast, if you delegate too much, you appear disconnected from what is going on in your department. Another very real danger is that you will lack the information necessary to make good decisions, making you appear indecisive. Over-delegation can also limit your ability to serve as an external conduit for information to the rest of the organization, making you appear uninformed.

A Leadership Continuum

Now that we understand the three basic archetypes, it is important to note that numerous points along the continuum combine the attributes of two different types of leaders.

For example, you may naturally employ more of a sage–sensei style of leadership. If the balance were 60/40 you would graph yourself as shown in Figure 2.2.

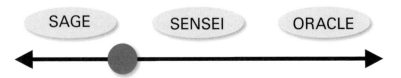

Figure 2.2. A sage–sensei style of leadership

An oracle–sensei with a balance of 70/30 is reflected in Figure 2.3.

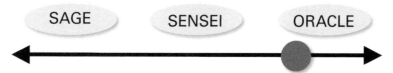

Figure 2.3. An oracle–sensei style of leadership

Remember, the various leadership styles are neither positive nor negative. Be honest with yourself as you think about what you feel is your dominant style of leadership. Also think about the key characteristics that others see in your behaviors and what this says about your leadership style.

Power Questions

- Where do you fall on the continuum?
- What conditions at work cause you to shift your leadership style?
- Does this tend to have a positive or negative effect on your team?
- Are you getting good results with the balance you currently exhibit?
- If not, what balance would you prefer to exhibit?

Becoming a Reflective Leader

You have been introduced to the various styles of leadership—the external expressions of your influence and knowledge. The next question that should come to mind is, "How can I benefit from the experience of others?"

We all realize the value of having mentors. They can help us identify our blind spots, and we can learn from their mistakes. Let's look at the Reflective Leader's Pyramid, which shows how data evolves into wisdom.

Step 1. Whether you realize it or not, as you interact with other leaders, you are constantly gathering a variety of data (Figure 2.4).

Figure 2.4. Result of collecting selected items from various data sources

Step 2. You can consciously or subconsciously benefit from other leaders' knowledge or learn from their experience to expand your own information base (Figure 2.5).

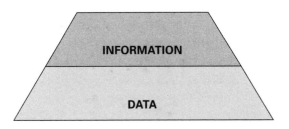

Figure 2.5. Result of placing data in meaningful context and conducting analysis

Step 3. In time, as you internalize and apply this knowledge, you will be able to use it in your own leadership experiences (Figure 2.6).

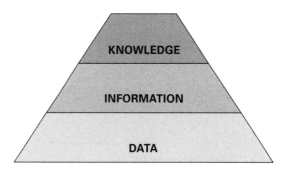

Figure 2.6. Result of internalizing information and then applying it to an intentional purpose

Step 4. The final stage of ownership occurs when you employ active reflection practices. Active reflection occurs through the three steps of thinking about an experience reflectively, discussing the lessons learned from it with a peer, and then identifying specific actions for improvement or growth. This strategy allows you to transform knowledge into wisdom (Figure 2.7).

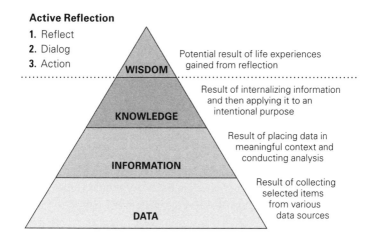

Figure 2.7. The Reflective Leader's Pyramid

To be a good reflective practitioner, you must develop strong inquiry skills—or, in other words, the ability to ask *powerful questions.*

Unfortunately, many times even good leaders never take this last step. They get so busy with the details of leading and managing that they forget they need to build their own leadership capacity. Remember, you can only continually develop the ability to help others by expanding your own abilities. This step is called "active reflection" because it requires a leader to think, discuss, and act.

Power Questions

- Have I ever practiced active reflection in the past?
- How do I build time into my schedule for active reflection?
- How do I provide opportunities for my staff to practice active reflection?

Application

Now we know more about the three leadership archetypes and how we can build a model for active reflection to learn about our practices. But how does this help you become more effective? The first question you need to ask yourself is, "Am I happy with the results I am getting from my team when I use my current leadership style?"

Yes, My Team Is on Fire

If the answer is *yes*, great—then you may not need to change much. However, no matter how good we are today, we should constantly look for ways to grow and improve. The biggest danger we need to avoid with high performing teams is assuming we can just put them on autopilot. Even the best of groups needs to stretch and grow. In this type of highly productive and positive environment, I suggest you use the LCM model (see Figure 2.1) to isolate the areas for growth to strengthen your current situation.

However, before you answer yes and happily move on, I challenge you with a couple questions.

1. While *you* are happy with the results you are getting, are your *team members* happy with the results they are getting?

2. Are your team members growing in their ability to shape and determine the type of results they get?

If you answered *no* to either question or to both, then you should reflect a bit more before moving forward. It sounds like you are on the right path, but good leaders always look for continuous improvement. You are probably already using more of the sensei model (or should be). If that is the case, then these questions are critical to helping you take the next steps in your journey toward effective leadership.

No, My Team Is Simmering

If the answer is *no*, don't despair—all of us have been there at some point in our careers. You can take several steps to heat things up. First reflect, "Are there specific situations where I am most concerned with my team's response to my leadership style?"

For most of us, emergency or crisis management situations are where leadership skills are tested most. Eventually, the data center will experience a crash, a natural disaster might hit, a widespread power loss could occur, or some other technology director's nightmare will rear its ugly head. It is during these periods that we need our staff's support the most. Unfortunately, during emergencies, they often see the side of us they least know how to work with or understand. As a result, they often do not know how to support us.

Many leaders' styles shift dramatically along the leadership continuum during times of extreme stress or change. The leader notices a corresponding change in reactions from his or her staff, and often the changed reactions are less than positive. If you find this to be the case, but you feel changes to your leadership style are necessary, then decide what actions you can take to help your staff understand your change in leadership style during those periods.

During periods of stress, technology leaders often default to the sage leadership archetype. They feel the need for a more directive and decisive role. Although the sage tends to be the default style in stressful scenarios, it is not the only effective style. The sensei style can be equally as effective in nearly any situation. In times of crisis, the oracle style is probably the most difficult to apply universally, unless there is an extremely disciplined second-tier leadership team in place. For the most extreme emergencies, my recommendation is that the oracle style of leadership should be used only if the technology leader is unavailable or is called upon to assume higher-priority duties.

The main leadership issue you should concern yourself with during high-stress periods is the fact that a shift in your leadership style is likely occurring. This discontinuity adds yet another variable to a period of great uncertainty. The fact that you are not leading your team in the way they are accustomed to will cause additional stress at a time when everyone can least afford it.

Another option is to make an effort to maintain the same leadership style you employ on a daily basis. Although this may seem counterintuitive, it actually provides the greatest sense of continuity for the organization and stability for your team. In times of uncertainty and chaos, your team will appreciate knowing what to expect from you. It allows your individual team members the freedom and confidence to move forward. They can employ their knowledge and talents to focus on solving the issue instead of trying to figure out *what you want* and *who you are.*

No, My Team Needs Some Heat

Going back to our original question: "Am I happy with the results I am getting from my team using my current leadership style?" If your answer is a simple *no*, then your team's problems are not situational (cropping up in emergency situations); they are the norm. You should take a hard look at the disconnect occurring between the needs of your team and your needs as the leader. This situation is the hardest to correct, but you can make dramatic improvements.

Here's a very common problem: Sometimes leaders and teams do not share common goals, or they unknowingly work toward different results. The first thing to establish is a shared vision, which we talk about at length in chapter 3. Once this alignment in vision occurs, you can move to the next step—aligning communication.

You must find what communication strategy is mutually beneficial. The flow of information is critical to reinforce ownership, respect, and a sense of community. Communication strategy is usually the area team members identify as the greatest deficiency from their leaders. Yet as leaders, we usually believe we consistently and effectively communicate to our teams. The conflict in perceptions is often gigantic.

Next, as a leader you must look at what engagement strategies you have developed for feedback and participation in the decision-making process. This area is one of the toughest to balance. There are decisions that can be delegated and others that can be debated and arrived at by consensus. And for some decisions, you must make the final call. Often, the team cannot differentiate among these decision types and will see them all as equal. However, if you have done a good job in the first three areas (ownership, respect, and sense of community), generally your team will trust your judgment in this matter.

Remember, a good leader must ensure several key strategies are in place.

- There is a shared understanding and ownership of the vision and goals.

- There are communication strategies the staff feels are valuable and effective.

- There are methods to engage the staff in decision making at the appropriate level.

Regardless of your personal leadership style, to succeed you need the support of your entire team. An effective IT organization is not built on the knowledge and ability of one person—*even you.*

Power Questions

- How would my team respond to the question, "Are we happy with the results we are getting now?"

- How would our customers (other departments, schools, etc.) respond?

- How different are the results now from a year ago? Two years ago?

- How is my leadership style affecting those results?

IT People Are from Jupiter

Some unique cultural and personality characteristics may exist within your team members, and you must understand them if you are going to be successful, regardless of your leadership style. The important thing to keep in mind is that people generally want to succeed and will be happiest as a part of a well-functioning team with a visionary leader. If you start with that premise, then you can learn to manage successfully the IT staff members' unique styles.

I am always hesitant to give out this type of advice, because it reminds me of those lunar calendars you can find in some Chinese restaurants. They talk about the different animal signs associated with each group of birth years and the characteristics of people who were born under those signs. Inevitably, as I read through them I think about different people I know and say to myself, "Wait, they don't fit that profile at all."

That is always the danger of generalizations—there will be many exceptions. But my experience has led me to some generalizations that I believe are quite useful.

Traditionally, district technology departments encompass three large groups: technical services, applications services, and instructional technology. The groups may go by different names; however, generally these are the broad categories that describe the largest functions most technology leaders have to manage on an ongoing basis. Obviously, the size and complexity of your district will have a bearing on how you will apply this material.

Why is this important, you ask? Remember the best seller, *Men Are from Mars, Women Are from Venus*? Well, generally speaking, IT people are from Jupiter. That is, they tend to have their own distinct set of cultural and personality characteristics. Actually, breaking it down further, each of the three groups tends to share certain characteristics distinct from the other groups.

Technical Services Staff

Technical services staff tend to be driven by the technology itself and may or may not understand their connection to the core mission of the district. They often enjoy exploring and playing with new technology on a regular basis.

They generally respond very well to the sage style of leadership because it is pretty cut and dry. Tell them what to do, and they will do it, as long as it meets some of their other needs listed above. They sometimes have a frustrating habit of putting off tasks they consider repetitive or boring. This is especially true if they already have another task that deals with a new or interesting technology, even if the other "boring" task has a higher priority.

A sensei can also be an effective leader of this group if he or she displays a level of technical content knowledge that is respected by the individual or team. With this knowledge, the sensei earns the right to mentor and coach the team on the "soft skills" such as customer service and team building.

Technical services staff often do not respond well to an oracle style of leadership. They tend to view the oracle as indecisive, and the oracle's characteristic disconnectedness is viewed—rightly or wrongly—as incompetence.

In the most efficient organizations, technical teams are highly motivated by monitoring their performance against metrics; thus, anything that drives efficiency is viewed as positive. However, in low-performing organizations, metrics will be less effective because the staff will block any form of accountability measure.

Technical staff usually prefer consistency, predictability, and stability. They seek regular recognition and are often competitive within their group. A sage will often foster this attitude, driving performance to an even higher degree.

They thrive on professional development that builds their technical skills but will push back on training designed to increase their interpersonal or soft skills. A sensei can overcome resistance through the earned respect of content knowledge, but an oracle may find their resistance very difficult to conquer.

Application Services Staff

Application services staff fall into two very distinct categories: *customer facing* and *developers*.

Application services staff who are customer facing (e.g., analysts and consultants) place a high value on relationships, both internal and external, and they are very protective of their customers. They work hard to articulate the needs of the customers and to ensure that the products and services delivered meet those needs. They do not react well when they perceive actions that endanger the customer relationship. Depending on their relationships within the team, this protectiveness can create volatile situations—analysts may feel like they are the customers' advocate; therefore, they must be right.

Developers—programmers especially—should never be allowed to see a customer (I say this partially in jest). They frequently value isolation and solitude. Their greatest joy comes from creating something from nothing or correcting the most difficult coding error. It is all about the program or product. They take great pride in their work and want personal recognition for it. Ironically, they may not want to be spotlighted and will often shy away from public attention of any kind. These cubicle dwellers are very hard workers and will often stay well past the time when others have left for the evening because they are captivated by the challenge of their task. They tend to be dedicated and committed as long as the work given to them is technically interesting.

The applications team tends to thrive in a culture of high flexibility and low structure. They generally respond well to an oracle style of leadership because this style meets their needs by identifying relationships as a priority and providing a high degree of isolation and delegation.

A sensei can also be very effective if he or she displays a level of development-content knowledge that is respected by the team. Only then does the sensei earn the right to mentor and coach on the soft skills.

Applications teams generally do not respond very well to sage styles of leadership because they feel rigidity and authoritarianism stifles their creativity. The sage's perceived lack of focus on customers is especially troubling for the customer-facing side of the team. They do appreciate the sage's ability to make a decision, though, when it comes to project milestones and dependencies, whereas this can be a problem for an oracle.

The application services staff is often the least understood in terms of their job function within the organization and even within the IT department. As result, they often feel undervalued and disconnected from the core mission of the organization. At the same time, they are usually some of the highest paid staff members in not only the department but in the district as a whole. This suggests that feeling valued is not just about salary.

The greatest conflicts often arise among the group in the area of tactical and strategic planning. The focus of some may be limited to delivery of the current product. They often do not look beyond that scope, resulting in rather linear and tactical thinking. This can even be true for the leader of the team. Others may be constantly thinking about how their products or services help the organization achieve its core mission. This core conflict can cause significant rifts within the team. The oracle and sensei are best suited to handle these issues. The sage can be challenged to bridge this gap because his or her focus is typically on completing the project at hand.

Instructional Technology Staff

The instructional technology staff is traditionally composed of former school-level staff: teachers who have been released from their duties to assist the district with integration of technology into the curriculum. They often still see themselves first and foremost as teachers. The group is most often led by a former principal, lead teacher, or library media specialist.

This team thrives under the leadership of an effective sensei because they are usually open to coaching and mentoring. They see this as an integral part of their job, so they welcome opportunities to participate in activities that show them how to be more effective. However, they still want a leader who can be decisive when there is a need to remove the obstacles that prevent them from accomplishing their jobs.

They generally respond well to an oracle who uses the style of direct-relationship leadership; they do not work as well with a leader who delegates too much. Team members desire a high degree of connection to their supervisor so they can stay in tune with what is going on. They require a strong communication channel with regular updates from across the department. They also can become easily frustrated if they feel decisions take too long to be made.

Technology instruction staff usually do not work well with a sage leader. First, as teachers they are used to a fairly high degree of autonomy within their classrooms and are not accustomed to having someone tell them exactly what to do. They also believe they are professionals and should, therefore, be able to exercise individual judgment. In other words, micromanagement often leads to an unhealthy team dynamic, although they may tolerate this style for brief periods or under unusual circumstances.

They have a low degree of tolerance for technical or procedural problems. If they think something is impeding instruction, they want it fixed or changed immediately.

Sometimes they may view the other members of the IT department as less professional, especially if the rest of the group is classified as staff rather than certified. (Sometimes you'll see the reverse: technical staff who view certified staff as "just teachers.") It takes careful management to ensure mutual respect. A sensei or relationship-oriented oracle can accomplish this balance. A sage may find managing this tug of war extremely difficult.

This team must value and build strong relationships with other departments within the district. They'll often want to serve on district committees and initiatives that are not directly related to technology; it's important to help them keep their priorities straight. The instruction staff believes a large portion of their time should be spent in the schools providing support directly to teachers.

Personal professional development is very important to this group. They want continual opportunities to grow in their craft as teachers and instructional technologists. When these opportunities are not present, they experience a high degree of frustration. If this negative attitude is not corrected in a timely manner, it can have a disastrous effect on the larger IT team, as the instructional technologists tend to be highly respected.

Power Questions

- How can I use these profiles to better understand my teams?
- What am I currently doing that is causing unintended effects within a particular team?
- Given my leadership style, what do I need to do differently for each team?
- What needs am I currently not meeting for each team?
- What needs am I currently doing a good job of meeting for each team?

Leadership is an intricate blend of science and art. Yes, there are numerous tools and strategies you can employ to improve your skill set. Yet leadership is about relationships, and those subtle dynamics cannot be quantified. Good leaders naturally tend to possess strong acumen for one side or the other, but they must constantly seek to develop their skills and maintain the fragile balance between different aspects.

True leaders must monitor the balance between task and relationship, confirm that each team member knows his or her role, guarantee that each member gets the right support, remove obstacles, and ensure everyone knows the direction of the group. In the end, the goals and results are what matter, and a good leader will make sure everyone on the team understands, owns, and celebrates them.

The Sensei's Parting Thoughts

- We learned there are three basic leadership archetypes in the Leadership Continuum Model—the *sage*, *sensei*, and *oracle*—each with unique leadership characteristics, strengths, and challenges.

- We saw that there are many points along the leadership continuum that combine the attributes of the archetypes.

- No leadership style is inherently positive or negative.

- We examined the Reflective Leader's Pyramid and how we move through its stages to become reflective thinkers and leaders.

- We learned how data evolves into wisdom and what is required from us as a leader to acquire wisdom.

- We looked at how to use results, the results you receive from your team, as a filter for determining what degree of change is necessary for a team and how your leadership style affects how changes will come about.

- We analyzed the specific characteristics of teams within a typical IT department, the leadership challenges, and the needs IT employees exhibit.

practical activities

In the previous section we looked at individual styles of leadership, talked about archetypes in the Leadership Continuum Model, discussed how to use these archetypes to better understand leadership style, and explored how personal style can help and hinder a leader's work with his or her staff.

The next section explores additional questions to consider regardless of where one might fall on the LCM continuum. Consider these introductory questions:

- What does your team or staff expect from you as the leader?

- How can active reflection help you be a better leader?

Activity 1 ■ What Is Your Role?

It is important to find out what your staff thinks your primary role or duties are as the technology leader. Your staff may quickly become frustrated if they do not have a clear understanding of your role and responsibilities. This phenomenon can be true within the ranks of your staff, as well. People on the same team sometimes have no idea of their coworkers' responsibilities and tasks.

One technique to help address this communication problem is a staff development activity to help people identify perceived versus actual job functions. This activity can be structured to focus on groups, individuals, or any functions you choose to select based on the level of trust that exists within your department. You can also alter this activity to fit the size of the group. The following activity is a great way to help your team understand the respective functions of their peers.

Instructions

1. Using Activity 1—Worksheet 1, have participants write their own job title in the appropriate blank. Using Table 1, have participants write in what they believe are the five most important functions of their job, based on their job description or other key evaluation tools.

2. Next, have participants complete Table 3, which relates to tasks that take a large percentage of their day but are ones they believe are not a part of their job function.

3. Depending on how you set up the activity, have everyone pass their worksheets clockwise.

4. The new person will fill in the first column for Tables 1 and 3. They should indicate whether they think those activities fall *inside* or *outside* the core function for that position as they understand it. They can also write in a function in Table 2 if they think there are things more important than what is listed in Table 1.

5. The rotation continues, with each person completing a column.

6. The rotation ends when the paper arrives back to the original participant.

7. You or the facilitator helps the large group discuss the findings.

ACTIVITY 1 ▪ WORKSHEET 1

What Is Your Role?

Job Title _____

Table 1. Identify the top five tasks that you believe are the key responsibilities or job functions for your position.

		1	2	3	4	5	6	7	8
	Inside								
	Outside								
	Inside								
	Outside								
	Inside								
	Outside								
	Inside								
	Outside								
	Inside								
	Outside								

Table 2. Are there any additional functions missing that should be in the top five?

Table 3. Identify the top five tasks that you spend a large percentage of your time doing that you view as *outside* your position responsibilities.

		1	2	3	4	5	6	7	8
	Inside								
	Outside								
	Inside								
	Outside								
	Inside								
	Outside								
	Inside								
	Outside								
	Inside								
	Outside								

Activity 2 ■ **Active Reflection**

Active reflection is one of the areas where all leaders can continually improve. By nature, most of us are *doers*. We are doing something, getting others to do it, or envisioning how to get it done. Unfortunately, in the process of doing, we usually spend very little time stepping back to see what *was done*. It is in this reflection that we often learn the most valuable lessons.

In classrooms we ask students to reflect on their work so they can improve the final product or process for the next time. This counsel would be wise for technology leaders to heed as well. It does occur, but in rare instances. In project management, in the customer acceptance phase following the sign off, this type of reflective activity is a vital stage of the process, a time when you debrief and document your learning. After an emergency, we sometimes postmortem the experience. We try to identify the situation's root cause and what should be done to prevent similar experiences in the future. Yet these types of learning opportunities are not often part of the everyday leadership routine.

One strategy for incorporating reflection into your normal workflow is to schedule it into your weekly conferencing activities or individual planning activities. As you meet with your direct reports for a weekly conference, take five to ten minutes and use Activity 2—Worksheet 1 to reflect together on the prior week. This process can be done in group or one-on-one sessions with your direct reports. It can also be a very beneficial activity for your own personal development. Active reflection can be a powerful tool for coaching and professional development.

To gain the full value of this approach, you must aim for a *call to action* and then build in an *accountability measure*. In this activity, you will see that action addressed in the *next steps* line item. It is especially important to include a due-by date to establish mutual accountability. Without it, this process becomes merely an interesting conversation.

You can use the same reflective process when you are doing your own individual planning for the week. Again, the key is to follow up on the *next steps* if you are going to realize the full value of the process.

Instructions

1. For each question, complete responses in each column. Pay special attention to the *next steps*, even for the success question.

or

1. Conference with participants about their responses, especially the *next steps*. Make sure to have due-by dates assigned in the *next steps*.

2. Follow up on the status of the *next steps* on the due-by dates to help reinforce the implementation of the desired action.

ACTIVITY 2 ▪ WORKSHEET 1

Active Reflection

	Top Success	Top Challenge	Top Loss
What was it? Describe what it was			
Why did it occur? Identify the key or critical factor(s) that was most important			
Lesson(s) Learned Describe the key "take away" for you personally			
Next Step(s) Identify what action you will initiate next as a result and by when			

chapter 3

what does
success look like?

Vision without action is merely a dream;
Action without vision just passes the time;
Vision with action can change the world.

Joel Barker, futurist

You probably have some notion of what success looks like for you and your team. But have you really thought about it? How will you recognize success if your picture isn't clear?

Max's Journey

As Max walked into his leadership class, he looked around at the other students scattered throughout and began mentally sorting them. The ones sitting in the back of the room were carrying on spirited conversations with each other, so he figured they might be good friends trying to knock out an elective.

He saw several people dispersed in various rows in the middle of the room sitting quietly. He pegged them as diligent, studious, no-nonsense types that were probably here to get the coursework done so they could meet a specific work-oriented requirement.

Then there was the final group. They sat in the front couple of rows and had their books in neat stacks with fresh notebooks or a laptop poised, ready to dive into the class. These were the ambitious, teacher's-pet types. For them, Max figured, this class was a stepping-stone in some lofty career goal; maybe for them it was less about learning and more about competition.

Max was not sure where he fit in with the other students at this point. However, he was excited about the prospect of learning, and he definitely was excited to study under Professor Sensei. He knew that the professor would be able to teach him a lot. So Max selected a desk in the center of the room about four rows back and began unpacking his materials.

Professor Sensei walked into the classroom and put his backpack on the desk. He then sat down on a tall stool. The students began to quiet down. He smiled at the class and spoke.

"'Begin with the end in mind.'

"These famous words are from the classic work, *The Seven Habits of Highly Effective People* by Stephen Covey. In this book, he proposes that one must have a clear picture of the desired outcome prior to initiating any action in order to achieve it successfully.

"As an effective technology leader, when you ask, 'What does success look like?' you are actually seeking to answer several key questions:

- What will be the result of delivering the final product or service?

- How will we know when it has been delivered in a manner acceptable to our customers?

- What criteria will we use to evaluate our effectiveness? Efficiency?

- How will this further the mission of the department or organization?

"There will be other questions as well. The key is being able to identify and answer the ones that will ultimately define the critical path necessary to ensure success. In this class, we will explore the role you have in using a vision to help you do just that. It is a critical skill to develop as you provide leadership in your organization or department."

Max settled in and began taking notes.

Theory

A key responsibility of any leader is the development and management of an organization's or team's vision. The presence of a powerful vision is what allows an organization to reach its goals.

mission — every day — what we do
Vision — future   For whom
*   benefit*

Who Has the Map?
The Role of Vision in an Organization

As educators, we usually gravitate toward common catch phrases like "create an educational experience where all students can learn and grow" or "successfully prepare all students for their future," which become the vision for our schools. These ideas are nice sentiments, although often clichés. Power only comes when the vision is translated into concrete actions, and that only happens when several important things occur within the organization:

- The vision is clear and compelling so that it inspires a desire to achieve it.

- All stakeholders understand and embrace the vision.

- The operational goals and objectives throughout the organization are aligned with the vision.

- The vision is omnipresent—constantly reminding people what they are working to achieve.

- The behaviors of the stakeholders clearly reflect the vision.

Can You Still See the Lighthouse? A Leader's Role

As technology leaders, you are responsible for developing and managing a vision. Based on your background, you may easily see that one facet of that vision speaks to how technology will positively transform the educational experience for all students. However, we must also realize our scope of influence reaches into all aspects of district operations, including, for example, the business functions. Regardless of your personal history, we must be sure that our vision encompasses the entire organization.

It is important to understand that all operational areas are merely support arms designed to allow the instructional staff of a school district to carry out the core mission. Therefore, when we apply technology effectively in administrative or operational areas, we are still impacting the educational experience, although in a less direct manner.

Another aspect to managing an organizational technology vision is ensuring tight alignment with the core mission of the district. It is only through this close alignment that the vision finds true significance and the ability to transform the educational process. Therefore, you need to be intentional with how it is managed. This requires a highly structured planning process—both initially and ongoing.

A final important component of the visioning process is building a vision for the department or team you supervise. As the leader for your group, regardless of its size, you must develop a vision that ensures the group can deliver upon the broader organizational technology vision. This departmental vision serves as the focusing lens for decision making, professional development, customer service, and the overall culture for your team.

Plan Is a Verb: The Vision Put into Action

As we said earlier, an ongoing structured planning process is critical to the development of a powerful and effective vision. Yet as the planning process matures, the vision must be transformed into action—that is where it gains relevance and form. Normally this transition occurs through the development of strategic goals and objectives. These are the working targets that identify the results you want to achieve on an annual or periodic basis and the evaluative measures you will use to see whether they were attained. The goals and objectives then evolve into operational action plans that drive the daily activities for the department.

This alignment develops synergy, allowing leaders to integrate day-to-day tactical work with their long-term strategic planning. In best practice, it enables leaders to incorporate the normal operational work into a performance management program for the staff. As a result, the department's evaluation system is also aligned with the key department goals and objectives.

Avoid having two different sets of criteria driving the performance for your staff; for example, make sure that the qualities for their annual staff evaluation are not competing with the department goals and objectives. Ultimately, you want your team to share responsibility and accountability for what you and your team are being evaluated on by your supervisor. This type of integrated model does that and allows your team to feel like they are making a significant contribution toward achieving the organization's or department's technology vision.

Power Questions

- What makes our organization's technology vision compelling and inspires others to achieve it?

- What makes our vision more than a cliché? *not just words / has goal, objectives, & strategies in place*

- What steps have you taken to integrate the operational and strategic aspects of the vision management process this year?

- Besides you, who else really owns the department's technology vision? How do their behaviors show it? *All stakeholde*

- How can we tighten the alignment of our technology vision to the district's core mission? To the department's vision?

- How omnipresent is our vision? *should be everywhere*

Critical Thinking
PS
Creativity + Innovation
Info lit
Comm
Social Resp
Collab

initiative
Self-direction

Application

In many organizations, moving from the abstract exercises of creating vision and goal statements to institutionalizing them can be daunting at best. As a result, the process often is left undone. The following section will explore simple ways you can take your guiding principles and make them a living part of your ongoing operations. Then they will begin to have a visible impact.

Developing Your District's Vision

When developing a vision, make sure the organization's employees:

- understand and embrace the vision
- use the vision to guide the way they set their goals for the year
- see the vision's effects in their work every day
- see the vision reflected in their behaviors and decision making

As discussed earlier, there are two distinct aspects to the technology vision that must tightly align:

1. The district's global vision for technology use as a strategic tool to impact teaching and learning

2. Your vision for the IT department/team as you support the broader district vision

Many documents can be found outlining the planning processes for creating vision statements. Therefore, I will not spend much time on that subject. However, several key ideas should be covered before moving on to developing the departmental vision, which usually receives less attention.

Feedback and Ownership

Most leaders know that strategic organizational visions must have broad-based support and ownership regardless of their content focus—technology or otherwise. Yet it is interesting how many times I review the technology committees for districts and find a narrow stakeholder list. This is a deadly first step for developing any type of strategic vision and should be avoided at all costs. There are numerous techniques for engaging stakeholders without assembling a committee of thousands.

The following are ideas for how to engage stakeholders:

- Host focus groups to examine key issues and allow discussion about only those topics.

- Employ listservs and moderated chat rooms where input can be solicited and collected. Analyze and publish the feedback in a public forum for review by your broader community so they know they were heard.

- Conduct small town-hall forums throughout your community and encourage staff members to attend and participate. This can help break down the barriers between staff and community.

- Ensure that the student community participates by meeting with student councils or student activity boards.

- Host a public access TV show where a panel facilitates a question-and-answer forum for a call-in event.

As you can see, there are many ways to break out of the traditional methods of gaining feedback and extending ownership. Remember your goal is for the final technology vision to be truly owned by the larger educational stakeholder community—not just your department.

Publicity and Ongoing Communication

Although communications will be covered in depth later in this book, a few concepts related to vision should be addressed here. Many times leaders fall into a deadly cyclic trap. They will develop a powerful, engaging vision and successfully sell it to the stakeholder community. Then it fades into the IT department only to reappear annually during the budget development cycle.

This pattern is a waste of time and energy. Worse, it deprives the stakeholder community of the opportunity to continue participating in, supporting, and championing the vision for technology in their schools. They forget about it in the midst of everything else that happens. So, a major part of your job as the technology leader is to create opportunities to promote, publicize, and report progress toward the vision and its associated goals. You must keep your accomplishments in front of everyone. That way, the vision stays in their consciousness, and they will remember why it is important.

The following are strategies to keep the vision front and center. Many of them are simple and require minimal time for returns on the investment.

- Develop a graphic organizer that clearly lays out the vision in layman's terms so interested parties understand not only what will happen but why it is going to happen. Remember, a picture is worth a thousand words.

- Create a method for providing consistent and engaging updates (e-newsletters, special Web pages, e-mail alerts, etc.) about progress on initiatives that are clearly aligned with the vision. The alerts should show what results have been achieved and why they are important to the stakeholders—not simply that the project was done.

- Create executive summaries for your technology vision and action plans that are easily understood. Distribute the summaries to key contacts and decision makers in your community, such as the chamber of commerce, city council, economic development council, county commissioners, and so on.

- Create a community-based technology advisory group that you provide updates to on a quarterly basis. Then solicit ideas from them about how to share your progress with the larger community.

- In order to keep moving forward, you must continue to generate positive energy and buzz about what is happening with the activities associated with the technology programs in your district. Success breeds more success. It also fosters greater levels of support—economic and otherwise—which, in times of diminishing financial resources, is critical.

The visioning process is not simply an intellectual exercise. Once the stakeholders accept a vision, they are emotionally invested, not merely fiscally or factually involved. They want you to succeed. Yet they also want to know you are adhering to the standard that inspired them in the first place. Be cautious when forming your vision because once community members accept a vision, they might become hesitant to deviate or revise the vision.

Monitoring and Evaluation

The final area I want to explore is the area most lacking in all strategic planning audits I have conducted: monitoring and evaluation. I must admit that as a technology leader, this is the area that I must continually challenge myself to develop. In today's climate of increased accountability and shrinking resources, this component becomes even more vital for long-term viability.

In developing your technology vision, you will begin to break it down into goals and objectives. For each of these units, go back to the original question, "What does success look like?" Although this may seem like a simple question, the answer can be rather complicated as you apply it to your strategic planning process.

The biggest shift technology leaders must make is to move from measuring the delivery of *products* or *services*, to measuring *results* as the indicator of success. The easiest way to understand the difference between the two types of outputs is to understand the question it answers: one answers *what,* and the other answers *why.*

The other part of a results orientation is building *quantitative* and *qualitative* measures as a part of the evaluation process. Since the end product or service is no longer the primary measure of success, you need new metrics for monitoring and evaluating what success looks like. Those

Sensei's Advice

- Products and services answer *what,* and results answer *why.*

- Creation of products or services alone—or answering the *what* question—will not guarantee movement toward achieving the vision. This is merely doing something new.

- Focus on the results—or answering *why*—and determine whether they were positive and relevant, thereby moving you closer to attaining the vision.

indicators must be defined during the initial planning process, not at the end. The advantage is that they have a positive impact on the way the implementation plan is designed and significantly increase the probability that you actually will attain them.

Finally, once you have built quality measurement metrics for your goals
and objectives, it is up to you and your team to create mechanisms to:

- monitor the fidelity of implementation

- collect the data necessary for measuring the metrics

- analyze and report attainment against targets

If you do not monitor and report results, then merely creating the
measures is an exercise in futility. However, if you take this process
seriously, it creates a wonderful feedback loop full of information that
makes the implementation of future technology plan initiatives easier,
more efficient, and more effective.

Using a structured strategic planning process for developing the
district's technology vision is critical for success. Yet to be an effective
technology leader, you must look beyond the process itself to other
aspects involved in the management. Issues such as broad stakeholder
ownership and feedback, ongoing publicity and communication, and
monitoring and evaluation need special attention if you want the plan
to have its full impact.

Power Questions

*School-based
survey
yearly*

- What were the last two new strategies you implemented
  to increase stakeholder feedback? How long ago was that?

*stakeholder
students are
role and expectation
of student*

- What roles do students play in developing, communicating,
  and monitoring your technology vision?

- Beyond the traditional methods of print and the Web,
  how do you communicate your technology vision to your
  community on an ongoing basis? How effective is it?
  How do you know? *PTA, Open House,*

- What evaluation metrics do you use for fidelity of
  implementation? What do you do with the results?
  Surveys

- What do you do if a current technology program does
not show positive instructional results, but it is in the
technology plan? How do you know today? *survey*
Goals, objectives
revise

Developing Your Department Vision

The second part of vision building for which you are responsible as
a technology leader is creating a vision for your immediate team or
department. In most leadership guides, this area receives little or no
attention. This omission is most unfortunate. This missing element is
why significant disconnects often occur between the strategic direction
of the IT department and the district as a whole.

As a result, you will inevitably see a department working at cross-
purposes with itself to accomplish different agendas. This lack of
unified focus leads to decreased effectiveness and less than stellar
results. It also causes the overall organization to question the value
of the IT department and its ability to perform. In the most severe
situations, it may even cause them to question the effectiveness of
your leadership and capacity to deliver the technology vision.

Putting Humpty Back Together: Begin with Alignment

One cannot overemphasize the importance of alignment. We talk
about it throughout this chapter with regard to vision, mission, goals,
and objectives. The same things hold true as you begin working
through the process for your department. Start this process by
developing a simple chart similar to the one shown in Table 3.1 (pg. 53).

The primary benefit of this chart is that it clearly lays out the alignment
between the department's guiding principles and the district's guiding
principles. As educational technology leaders, it is always important to
remember our primary role is that of supporting the school or district's
core function: teaching and learning. For many staff members it can be
difficult, if not impossible, to make that connection based on the jobs
they do on a daily basis.

For them, it is easy to get wrapped up in the complexities and flash of the technology world and forget the guiding mission. The representation of guiding principles' alignment in Table 3.1 is a great reminder that IT goals are secondary to the larger goals of the organization. It also helps reinforce the idea that the department or school goals must be aligned in a way that supports the larger organization goals.

Your employees must not only understand this connection, but also communicate it as they go about performing their duties in the school or district. Otherwise, no matter how interesting or important the projects are, their efforts may be viewed as at cross-purposes to the rest of the organization.

This misalignment is why many IT departments find themselves constantly battling to defend the value they offer and the need for continued funding. So how do you win the battle?

1. Ensure the IT vision, activities, and priorities are aligned to the core mission of the district.

2. Clearly and regularly articulate this alignment to the employees within the department and the stakeholders outside it.

When you do both of these things, battles are minimized.

How do you get your employees to actually think about the mission regularly?

There are several ways you can engage them in thinking about the information until it becomes something they own. First and most importantly, they must be involved in the development process. Nothing can substitute for emotional buy-in on a product that they helped build. When you are first putting the information and tools together, ensure that your employees are a part of the process.

Table 3.1. A visual representation of the alignment between a department's guiding principles and a district's guiding principles.

School District Mission Statement	Supporting students to achieve their life goals by providing them the necessary skills.
Vision for the District Technology Department	"We are respected and valued as competent, caring professionals who partner with our community to develop, deliver, and support technology solutions that transform teaching and learning for all students."
Motto	*Whatever It Takes*
IT Department Values	Improving teaching and learning is job one.
	Excellence is the gold standard.
	Teamwork is great work.
	Respect is given to all.
	Quality customer service is key to success.
	Learning is for everyone.
Proposed Department Goals for the Current School Year	Positively impact students' educational experiences through increased opportunities for leadership and demonstration of learning.
	Deliver a customer-support model that effectively and efficiently meets their needs while also communicating genuine caring.
	Develop and provide new technology tools and resources, making the instructional process more meaningful for all persons involved.
	Continue building the culture of a "learning community" within our department.
	Actively work to build healthy partnerships throughout the district in order to better serve our customers.

Another advantage of a tool like Table 3.1 is that it makes a great wall chart for employees—a visual reminder of the big picture. It is so easy to get bogged down in daily activities and problems. Using this tool, you can constantly remind them of the greater purpose they are helping to achieve, which in turn is good for increasing employee morale and motivation.

You might want to dress the wall chart up with attractive graphics and color to make it visually appealing. Then make copies readily available to all staff members to post in their work areas. Also make oversized posters that can go up in high traffic areas such as break rooms or hallways.

Although these strategies may not sound like traditional technology leadership activities, remember you are not working in a traditional IT environment. The rules are different, so you must lead differently. However, it is easy to see how these practices would be equally effective in any IT environment. Your staff needs to understand, own, and act on the vision regardless of what type of organization you are leading.

Power Questions

- How many of your employees can articulate the district's strategic goals?

- What strategies do you currently use to make the connection for your staff between your department/team goals and the larger organization goals? Are they effective? How do you know? *PD, Web, Writer*

- How many executive cabinet members can articulate your department's vision?

Are We on the Same Page? Department Values

As mentioned previously, vision is more than just the vision statement. One of the characteristics of an effective vision is that it must evoke a strong emotional appeal or promote a sense of passion about the outcome. Values are the heart of a vision; they define who we are as an organization or department. They also are clear indicators of what is truly valued within a school or department.

Often we articulate one set of values, and then our actions and decision making loudly proclaim something quite different. This is why it is important to have this discussion within the department. We send a message with each action we take or decision we make. Is the message the one we intend?

The "Defining Values" technique is a simple way to outline clearly what is important to your department or team. It is necessary to understand these values are professional and not personal. Defining and shaping personal values are usually beyond the

Sensei's Advice

■ When writing your value statements, they should be clear and concise.

■ If there are too many words or if you have too many value statements, no one, including your employees, will remember them.

scope of our role as an employer. In this venue, we are really talking about what characteristics define the professional behaviors of our staff as they work to fulfill their duties.

People often ask, "Do you draft the value statements or let the group do it?" There is no set rule here. It depends on where you are with your staff members. If you have built a culture with a high level of trust, it will not really matter, as they will support either direction you choose.

If, on the other hand, there is a great deal of anxiety and distrust, you will need to increase the level of involvement by your staff members. Otherwise, the statements will become your values and not theirs. The end result in that situation will be no change in behaviors or culture.

Regardless of which situation you are in, one suggested approach is to create a draft set of values and then take it to your group for discussion and revision. The one rule I strongly advise is to ensure that the values critical to achieving the core vision established for the department are included on the list. Remember as the leader, *you* are ultimately responsible for managing the vision and achieving the goals, not the staff.

In Figure 3.1 you see a sample values document. These statements identify more of who you want to become than who you necessarily are today. You will also notice they are open to broad interpretation. This is intentional because the goal is to strive for group ownership, and ownership comes through discussion.

---

core values:
defining who we are   **we believe that...**

Values are more than merely catchy phrases on a wall or in a strategic plan. They are reflections of the organization's character and direction, which are ultimately defined by the actions of the people within it.

Improving teaching and learning are core.

Excellence is the standard.

Equal commitment, collaboration, and celebration make us a great team.

As we move into the next phase of development as a department, it is vital we understand and embrace the core values that will drive the process. Understanding is the first step in becoming mobile reflections of the values, and embracing the values is to watch them live.

Students are partners in our progress.

Exceptional customer service is key to success.

We are a community of learners.

Figure 3.1. A sample values document
Used with permission of the Kent School District, Kent, WA.

Imagine the following scenario: You are meeting with a group of your staff members. One moderate or lower performing staff member may ask, "What exactly does *excellence* mean? Won't that depend on who you are talking to?" This is a great lead-in question. It provides the opportunity for one of your superstars to talk about what excellence means to them. It is also a wonderful way to allow your high performers to describe what they do and why it is important to them and their customers. You can glean concrete examples of best practice from within your team to highlight or emphasize the key concepts in the values.

Another positive aspect of this method of allowing peer-to-peer discussion is that it takes you out of the role of always trying to explain or sell the concept to reluctant staff members. It is in these discussions you can get at the real change issues you are trying to address, and it helps when you aren't doing it alone.

Mentioned previously, when you have finalized your values list, you want to create a visually appealing way to display the values. Then distribute the list to the staff—they need to see it daily. If they don't see the values, they can't live them. Change takes time and regular reinforcement. You will also need to build these values into your staff evaluation process if you want to see long-term systemic change.

Remember, what you are seeking is change in culture. You want your staff to achieve their goals while also demonstrating the behaviors that embody the values. Let's say that again: you want them to meet their goals while emphasizing your department's values. Remember what was said earlier about our words and actions often being out of sync. This point could be the most important idea in this chapter. You want your team to do the right things in the right ways. This may very well be the most difficult sell you will have as leader.

Power Questions

- What values do your team's actions communicate today?

- What values do you want your team to be known for in the district?

- What changes have to occur within the team for these values to be realized? What changes have to occur in you for this to happen?

- What obstacles prevent you from doing this now? How can you remove them?

Are We There Yet? Good to Great

In the recent best seller, *Good to Great: Why Some Companies Make the Leap ... and Others Don't*, author Jim Collins studies what allowed certain Fortune 500 companies to make the transition from merely *good* to *great*. Although many of us wish we could just achieve *good*, I challenge you to strive for greatness, as it is within your grasp. There are simple steps you can take to begin this journey.

The first thing to remember is that almost no one gets up in the morning and comes to work thinking, "I am going to make sure to do a really mediocre job today." The vast majority of employees honestly set out to do the best job they can. As the leader responsible for them, you have to start with that belief about your staff members and peers if you want your organization to make that leap to greatness.

Second, you must help each person make the connection between his or her individual actions and the results achieved, or not, for the department. These individual actions either help or hurt. There is no neutral position. Many employees honestly think because of where they fall within the organizational hierarchy that what they do really does not make that much difference—good or bad. They also believe they have little control over helping to make things better.

Understanding these two principles, you can then begin to establish a meaningful context for dialogue within your team. Using a tool similar to the one in Figure 3.2, you can begin exploring how these concepts can help your team become more successful.

Table 1. Moving from *good* to *great* begins with understanding what you currently do that rises to each level, and what the differences are between the two.

What is one thing that I do great within my job?	
What is one thing that we do great as a department?	
What are the things that we do as a department that are good?	
To be great, what are some things we should abandon or phase out as a department and why?	

Table 2. For our department to go from *good* to *great*, what changes would it take from…?

Our clients	
Department management	
My co-workers	
Me	

Figure 3.2. Building cultures of greatness exercise

This model is different from most change improvement activities that you may have reviewed. It is focused on a positive expectations model.

When we begin by focusing on strengths instead of deficits, a very different type of conversation occurs. This approach allows you to focus on the positive aspects of your staff's current performance. This is a very important point. If you seek to increase the sense of efficacy within your staff members, you should always strive to do it inside a positive framework. It minimizes many of the defensive postures they will bring with them, which can prevent authentic dialogue and reflection.

Far too often in processes like these, we begin with statements such as, "What do we need to change?" or "What should we do better?" The obvious implication is that something we are doing now is wrong or not done well. Instead, by identifying what they are doing that is great, they will think about what strengths the department already possesses. Strength is necessary to make change possible, and believing that change is possible is the first step toward efficacy.

A subtle aspect of the exercise is the sequence of reflection. In Figure 3.2, Table 1, the questions start with the individual and work outward to the team or organization. This allows the individuals to feel good about themselves and the team before asking any questions about change. The tool is designed to increase each team member's sense of self-efficacy.

Like it or not, when it comes to change, we are often more concerned about our own well-being than other people's welfare. It is vital to have the team think about how they can positively contribute to the changes that you are bringing about in this alignment and visioning process. What they need to understand is what value they bring to the group, especially if you are shifting direction. This exercise gives them the chance to identify greatness first for themselves and then for the group.

Table 2 reverses the order, providing a safety zone. This is important while each individual is processing conflicting thoughts about what is already working well and what needs to change. The tool starts with customers and works backward to the individual team member. This reduces the initial anxiety, since we can identify what someone *else* should change to make things better for us. Eventually, the tool does get down to what the individual must change to help achieve greatness.

So, when you begin discussions around the change agenda within your school or department, why not start from the positive?

Power Questions

- What was the last thing your team accomplished that you thought was great? Why do you consider it great?

- What would your customers say you and your team do that is great?

- What would your team say you do as a leader that is great? What do you want to be known for as doing a great job on? By your team? By the organization? By the community?

The Sensei's Parting Thoughts

- We looked at the need for you to provide clear leadership in developing a technology vision for your organization and your department or team.

- We discussed the critical need for alignment of the district's educational vision and the department's vision for the effective use of technology in order to ensure effective use of resources and a clear direction.

- We looked at three key components that technology leaders must manage within the organizational vision: feedback and ownership, publicity and ongoing communication, and monitoring and evaluation.

- We also examined the role of values as an important part of supporting a departmental vision.

- We talked about ways to move your team from *good* to *great* as you work to lead them in understanding and owning a vision.

There is no magic here. The tools and strategies in this chapter are not rocket science or even that innovative. However, the thought process behind them will allow you to expand your understanding of how to manage the vision within your school or district.

As you work with these tools and strategies or create your own, remember what you are really trying to accomplish:

- You want your vision to be understood and embraced by your staff and customers.

- You want the vision to shape where your department is going this year in terms of its goals and ensure those goals are closely aligned to the core mission of the school district.

- You want the vision evidenced daily by your staff members and colleagues as they shape the educational experience for the students.

- You see the vision reflected in the tangible action plans and behaviors of your staff.

- You want to see your team strive for continuous improvement, driven by the department's value, goals, and vision.

Remember, if your vision is not paired with action, it is merely an unattainable dream.

practical activities

Activity 3 ■ **Situational Gap Analysis**

This activity is useful as you begin developing the departmental vision. It is designed to be done in two parts: Exercise One and Exercise Two. You can easily adapt these exercises to work with a small subset that includes only your IT leadership team, if the size of your technology operation allows for that. The activities are scalable to include a full department participating in small work groups, as well.

Many times staff members tend to see only the obstacles that prevent the department from accomplishing their objectives, goals, or long-term vision. The following approach allows you to help them focus on what they *can* do. The challenge is getting everyone to see that there is a gap and that there are actions within their scope of control they can do to build a bridge.

helpful hints

- *The first time you go through this exercise, you may find the discussion becomes fairly high-level or abstract. It may also be shallow, or it may range all over the board, covering any number of issues both on- and off-topic.*

- *Regardless of the type of feedback generated, it is important to capture it all.*

- *The duration of the exercise should allow for generating specific, actionable strategies that can be done both as a team and individually to move across the gap.*

EXERCISE ONE

The key to making this exercise work is having participants focus on the current reality without making a value judgment about it. It is neither positive nor negative—it just is. Instead, provide three specific filters to help broaden their thinking: *technical, cultural,* and *instructional.*

What you will find is different people will naturally focus on the areas in which they have the most expertise. This narrowing of perspective is a very reasonable reaction. However, encourage them to stretch beyond their comfort zone.

Instructions

1. Divide participants into small groups and provide a copy of Activity 3—Worksheet 1 (Situational Gap Analysis: Reality and Vision) for each person.

2. Allow quiet time for each participant to answer the questions.

3. Have the small groups discuss the findings, asking them to look for common ideas and strategies. Remember, the goal is to engage them in talking and thinking about the gaps in a meaningful way.

4. Ask the small groups to report their findings to the larger group.

5. Consolidate the information and provide a copy for use in the follow-up session.

EXERCISE TWO

The worksheet for this session was designed to drive the discussion in a more structured way. It talks about your role, as leader, in the visioning process and the responsibility you have. But the focus is on the individual team members this time, not you as the leader. One of the critical outcomes for this exercise is moving the team toward internalizing the vision. You want them to reflect on a more personal level instead of a global one.

The last question is the most important part of the exercise in that it calls for a personal commitment to action. It also gives a time frame—a very generous one—but one that still provides a sense of accountability.

Instructions

1. Before conducting this follow-up session, provide the group with the consolidated information from Exercise One.

2. Divide participants into small groups and provide Activity 3—Worksheet 2 (Situational Gap Analysis: Leader and Team Members) for each person.

3. As you begin, it is vital you share how important this activity is to you personally and that you want them to take it seriously. As you look over the worksheet, you will see why I am giving you this direction.

4. You also need to let the participants know at the beginning of this session that you intend to collect their responses to the final question and will be distributing them to the full team at a future time. This notification is a critical step in the process.

5. Allow quiet time for each participant to complete questions 1–4. **Tell them not to answer question 5 yet.**

6. Have the small groups discuss their findings, asking them to look for common ideas. This time you want them to focus on the importance of a shared vision.

7. Provide more quiet time and have each participant complete question 5.

8. Collect the worksheets from the participants at the end of the session.

9. Later, after you have reviewed the responses, aggregate the answers to question 5 into one document. Then distribute this document back to the full team that participated in the session.

This last step, while potentially scary, is very important in reinforcing the significance of your team's commitment to the vision and to the action steps designed to achieve your goals. It is also a critical part of the accountability model and the internalization process.

ACTIVITY 3 ■ WORKSHEET 1

Situational Gap Analysis: Reality and Vision
EXERCISE ONE

The *situational gap* is the distance between today's reality and our vision for tomorrow.

Please share your thoughts by answering the following questions:

1. What is creating that gap today?

2. Is it technical, cultural, and/or instructional?

3. What can we do to bridge that gap?

4. What is your vision for your team?

ACTIVITY 3 ▪ WORKSHEET 2

Situational Gap Analysis: Leader and Team Members
EXERCISE TWO

As we have discovered, sometimes the situational gap occurs because of factors such as technical limitations, cultural constraints, or instructional deficits. Sometimes, however, the gap occurs because the leader does not possess or articulate a clearly defined vision for the group he or she leads. When this is the case, it limits the leader's effectiveness in bringing about sustainable change.

This activity will help the leader identify the gaps between what he or she sees as the team vision and what the team members feel is the vision.

Please share your thoughts by answering the following questions:

1. What do you see as your primary role(s) within the department? Within your team?

2. What is the vision for your team as it relates to our department?

3. Why is this vision important?

4. What difference will it make in student achievement?

5. How will you go about achieving this vision? What are some of the specific enabling strategies you intend to use in the next two years?

Activity 4 ■ **Measuring Success: Moving from Activities to Results**

In education we spend a lot of time measuring activities to determine success. Many educators have made the shift to measuring outputs already; however, we tend to look only at the products or services created. Some districts may even evaluate the quality of the effort expended in the creation of the products or services. Unfortunately, we are still missing the mark if we stop there.

The goal has to be to evaluate the results in terms of impact on the organization (the *why* or *so what*). When we can clearly identify what difference was made by having expended the effort and resources on a project, only then can we say what success looks like.

The next activity takes a traditional business production model and divides the cycle into three phases. It then provides examples of functional areas of operations for the business to show what the inputs and activities would be in the production cycle. Finally, it shows what outputs (results) would be yielded in the cycle.

This same model is then applied to a typical educational environment. The goal is to identify what the outputs/results are for each functional area. You can expand this activity by applying the same model to your IT functions or projects.

This activity forces participants to go beyond thinking about the activities as the results. It helps them focus not on the product or service delivered but instead on what the product or service does for the organization. This way of thinking is a major shift for many educational organizations and IT departments.

After using the model to analyze one or more facets of your program, engage your staff in a discussion about the observations. Discuss how focusing on results will change the way you build metrics for measuring success.

Instructions

1. Lead a discussion about the basic business production cycle model to ensure participants understand the introductory graphic.

2. Lead them through the sample in Table 1 on Activity 4— Worksheet 1, relating it to the business production model. Make sure they make the connections between *inputs, activities,* and *outputs* (results).

3. Ask participants to spend time independently trying to complete Table 2 (using either an education or IT example).

4. Have participants work in small groups, sharing their ideas. Ask them to get consensus for the answers in their groups. Have them share their findings with the larger group.

5. Lead a large group discussion: How would project evaluation metrics change for your department or organization with this new way of thinking about results?

ACTIVITY 4 ■ WORKSHEET 1

Measuring Success:
Moving from Activities to Results

Using the information provided in the diagram below, identify outputs (results) appropriate for public education as they relate to your department.

Value Added

INPUT → ACTIVITIES → OUTPUT

Table 1. Typical private industry examples

Input	Activities	Output
Materials	Training	Increase production rates
People	Organizing	Decrease operating expenses
Budget	Planning	Increase sales per year
Equipment	Coordinating	Provide quality customer service
Time	Developing	Increase revenue earned

Table 2. Educational organization examples

Input	Activities	Output
Materials	Training	
People	Organizing	
Budget	Planning	
Equipment	Coordinating	
Time	Developing	

chapter 4

how will this improve
teaching and learning?

Learning is not attained by chance;
it must be sought for with ardor
and attended to with diligence.

Abigail Adams, 1780,
First Lady of the United States of America

Now we come to the most important chapter in this
entire book. I am equally as confident that it will be one
of the most controversial. Some of you will read through
this introductory section and immediately think, "This
is an utter waste of paper and ink," and proceed to skip
to the next chapter. Others of you will think, "I finally
have hit a chapter that I care about!"

No matter where you fall in the spectrum, my advice to you is to *read this chapter if you want to keep your job.*

As technology leaders, whether we come from private industry into education or emerge from the classroom trenches, we already realize that technology is changing the face of education in the classroom. However, technology must work in tandem with the instructional reform efforts already occurring within the district, or we will feel like Sisyphus rolling the boulder up the hill—we will never reach our goal.

I often see two positions on this issue. Technology leaders get enamored with the newest gadgets and software upgrades. Teacher leaders build their instructional technology silos separate from the district's core instruction department. The end result, or lack of results, is the same. Neither group has a broad-based impact on changing the educational experience for all students.

When you walk into a typical classroom in this country, it often still looks essentially the same as at the beginning of the technology revolution. Yes, it may house more computers and other technology devices, and perhaps they are connected to the Internet. Yet on a national scale, the types of instructional activities students are engaged in and the quality of these activities are on the whole markedly unchanged. True, you will find pockets of brilliance in nearly every district, but would you buy a house that had adequate lighting in only a couple rooms?

Is it really our responsibility as technology leaders to address this type of disconnect? Can we cope with these large-scale system issues when we lead only one particular department? Is that really our role? You will uncover the answer to those questions as you explore this chapter.

Theory

In this section, we are going to cover several basic principles for instruction and how technology is changing the picture in education. You might call this the ten-minute master's degree in education. We will look at elements of curriculum alignment, technology and instructional delivery, brain-based learning, and curriculum and instructional materials.

Curriculum Integration as the Goal

If you ask nearly any teacher how technology should be used in the classroom, the response would probably be, "Technology should be used as a tool to support instruction." Yet if you probe for a deeper understanding as to what that means or what that looks like in practice, then all of a sudden the answers are not nearly as clear. The issue becomes even more problematic when you begin talking about information literacy, the 21st-Century Skills framework, visual literacy, and other concepts that delve deeply into the ways technology should be manifested within the instructional experience.

Sensei's Advice

If any of the concepts mentioned in this chapter are foreign to you, then check out these useful URLs:

- enGauge 21st Century Skills: www.metiri.com/features.html

- From Now On— educational technology journal: http://fromnowon.org

- Kathy Schrock's Guide for Educators: http://school.discovery.com/schrockguide/

If you want to provide quality leadership to serve your organization, you need to broaden your knowledge base constantly, regardless of your background.

Many instructional or curriculum departments talk about technology integration as a goal. For them, this means including technology skills or concepts in the core curriculum areas. They often turn to the instructional technology team to provide the expertise needed to accomplish this task. The process still tends to be viewed as an add-on to the district's core curriculum development process. As a result, technology integration is often considered supplementary or not required in many districts.

Effective curriculum integration includes multiple components that must work together:

- Addressing the strategic instructional goals

- Aligning the instructional materials (electronic and nonelectronic)

- Developing standards-based assessments

- Monitoring fidelity in lesson delivery

In this model, technology resources are not treated any differently from other instructional resources. Yet they do provide special instructional benefits when applied appropriately. The instructor must also be acutely aware of classroom management issues to ensure this alignment occurs.

Classroom management includes but is not limited to:

- Identifying for the students the purpose for the lesson's inclusion of instructional standards or outcome(s)

- Using lesson plans and assessment instruments that effectively incorporate technology

- Making decisions around grouping strategies for students (for example, will they work in pairs or independently?)

- Shifting the role that students play in the learning process from passive learners to active creators

Power Questions

- When was the last time you had a discussion about curriculum and instruction during an IT staff meeting?

- How familiar are you with information literacy? Visual literacy? The 21st-Century Skills framework?

- What are the strategic goals of the Curriculum and Instruction Department for this year?

Changing Strategies

Effective curriculum integration also requires a dramatic change in the delivery strategies or methodologies used in the classroom. This area can be one of the biggest obstacles to practical implementation of technology on a wide scale in school districts. The need for new forms of knowledge representation, expanding means of communication and collaboration, and supporting reflection cannot be supplied by traditional teaching methodologies. However, there are multiple teaching models where technology can add significant value to the instructional process.

Anchored Inquiry

In this teaching approach, technology is the launch point for students as they use information in problem solving. Technology then serves as the anchor or catalyst to move the learner from a singular event to multiple thematic issues or questions on which the actual lesson can focus.

For example, a teacher uses a video clip from a popular film to engage the students and provide the background context prior to beginning the class discussion for a particular curriculum focus. Then the discussion will branch into a thematic, issue-driven focus within one or more content areas (Figure 4.1).

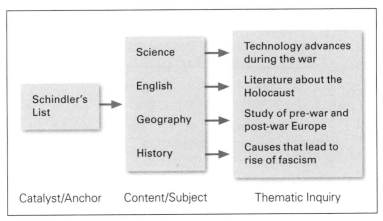

Figure 4.1. Anchored inquiry teaching approach

Project-Based Learning

Project-based learning allows technology to assist students in translating the theoretical into actual practice. This translation can take the forms of graphing, simulation, field research, media creation, and so forth. Technology can also play a valuable role in the assessment process, both summative and formative. The goal is to allow the student to demonstrate mastery of their learning, and technology can provide numerous ways to accomplish this goal.

Project-based learning:

- is problem-centered and solution-focused

- encourages teamwork and classroom support

- allows the students to work with actual sample data and data collection

- allows for continuous quality improvement on the part of the teacher and student

Technology also shifts the focus of control from the teacher to the student. The instruction is not only student-centered but often becomes student-directed. It is in this process that the level of student engagement increases, which in turn increases motivation and ultimately achievement. This potential for change is one of the key value-adds that technology brings to the instructional process.

Brain-Based Learning

An emerging domain in teaching pedagogy is brain-based learning. You will find this is new to many educators, too, so don't be surprised if they are not familiar with it. Brain-based learning studies the student's acquisition of knowledge in terms of understanding how the brain works best in instructional situations. The emphasis is on maximizing learning by understanding how connections and patterns are formed in the brain.

There are three dominant teaching delivery practices:

1. **Traditional Teaching.** In this type of teaching situation, teachers are in charge. They use traditional teaching strategies such as memorization, lecturing, rote memorization, and testing. This is generally the "old-factory model" of instruction where one-size-fits-all. It is probably the model that most of us went through as students.

    Technology would play a minimal role. Most likely it would take the form of drill and practice applications for students and possibly PowerPoint presentations to support teacher lectures and minimal productivity uses.

2. **Innovative Teaching.** In this type of teaching situation, teachers are still largely in charge of the classroom. However, they are reasonably comfortable with innovation and change, using various learning strategies and methodologies. The teachers see new possibilities for defining subject matter and assessment.

Technology would generally play a supplemental role. For students, it may be used to perform online research and to create word-processed reports and PowerPoint presentations. Teachers would extend their use to manage the full scope of administrative functions as well as instructional presentations. They will also bring in multimedia components to increase student engagement.

3. **Brain-Based Learning.** In this type of teaching and learning situation, learning becomes a collaborative process. Time constraints are flexible and students have a well-defined sense of where they want to go with their learning. Teachers draw on a vast array of teaching and learning strategies and emphasize ongoing questioning, expert assistance, and critical analysis.

   Technology plays an integral and transparent role. Students use the technology tools on a just-in-time basis to accomplish their work. They make critical decisions as to what resource is most appropriate for the task. Besides the previously mentioned functions, teachers will use technology to manage their teacher-student interactions, monitor student performance, and for assessment activities.

Obviously, the teaching models are much more involved than they are outlined here. Also there are many other aspects as to how technology would be used in each scenario. However, this brief overview is designed to provide you with an example of the developmental progression that occurs with changes in the teaching models.

You will notice that changes occurred for both the teacher and students. That is because teaching and learning is a relationship-based system. So if you change one factor, the other one will automatically be affected, whether the change was positive or negative.

Power Questions

- How could you use the information in this section to open dialogue with your Curriculum and Instruction Department?

- How can you use the information in this section to lead your team differently?

- Using this information, what changes should you make in your current approach to professional development?

The Third Leg of the Stool: Curriculum and Instructional Materials

In educational theory, the three legs of the stool are *instruction, assessment,* and *curriculum*. Instruction is what is actually taught in the classroom, assessment is what is tested, and curriculum is the formal guidelines or standards for what should be taught. In the previous section, we talked about instructional models and what it means to integrate technology into the curriculum. How are the curriculum and other instructional materials actually selected or adopted?

The Instructional Services Department retains primary responsibility for selecting and approving (adopting) the core instructional materials to be used in the classrooms. This includes the textbooks, the assessments (tests), curriculum (lesson standards and guides), and most supplemental or support materials. This curriculum selection and adoption process provides a high degree of control over what changes in instructional practice can and cannot occur. Teachers are generally held accountable for teaching the district's prescribed curriculum and using its adopted materials.

This structured, traditional approach to curriculum development and adoption can be problematic when it comes to introducing technology-based instructional materials into this cycle, especially when technology-based resources are proposed as replacements for existing materials. You will find that many existing organizational structures create barriers. These can be regulatory, political, or cultural.

For example, many states have laws that limit or exclude the adoption of technology-based or electronic materials in lieu of traditional textbook or basal materials. Even if not banned outright, many local districts' policies or practices do not make it easy to accommodate technology. As a result, many school districts will not venture outside traditional parameters when it comes to the definition of instructional resources.

There is also an issue of territorial control that often comes into play in many districts. Because adoption of curriculum resources, electronic or traditional, is viewed as a curriculum or instruction issue and not a technology issue, a turf war often ensues. Rather than build bridges of collaboration, departments will rally their political capital to reinforce long-held boundaries built on organizational structure. When this occurs, technology once again becomes an add-on to the instructional process, which then has to compete for the teacher's attention with numerous other demands in the instructional day.

The real win comes when a district tears down the walls and integrates its intellectual, fiscal, and political capital for the good of the students and staff. Educational technology can then be leveraged as a powerful instructional resource to support curriculum, assessment, and instruction. It does not become an ancillary appendage, but a core internal organ necessary for a strong-functioning system.

Power Questions

- ▪ How do you currently participate in the review and adoption of district instructional materials?

- ▪ What is your state law regarding the adoption of electronic instruction materials in lieu of basal materials? What laws exist regarding using electronic instruction materials as a supplement to basal materials?

- ▪ How does your selection of electronic instructional materials align with district academic standards? Beyond vendor claims, what review process ensures alignment?

- How does your selection of electronic instructional materials align with your student and staff technology competencies? What review process ensures alignment?

- How does your current install base of electronic instructional materials support your district's preferred assessment strategies? If it doesn't, what are you doing about it?

- What role do students have in the review and selection of district-wide electronic instructional materials? If none, why not?

Application

Now that you have a context for understanding the instructional environment in which technology must add value, the question becomes, "What exactly is my role as a technology leader?" The answer varies depending upon your individual background, your organization's expectations, and the alignment of your position.

Staking Out Your Role: Becoming an Instructional Partner

Even if you come from more of a technical background, you do not get to exempt yourself; you must still actively engage in shaping and providing leadership in this important domain. Some of the best examples of instructional innovation and transformation originated from outside curriculum services. But these educational changes are not sustainable long term without cooperation and buy in from important partners.

The type of leadership we will be talking about in this section is more strategic in nature and less about instructional pedagogy and content expertise. As a result, except in rare cases, this material will not differentiate between technology leaders that come from technical or instructional backgrounds.

Make Sure You Are at the Table

To be a part of the educational change process, you must be in the discussion from the beginning and all the way through implementation. There will be times when you may be only an observer, actively learning from the other members of the team. This is a great time to ask clarifying questions, demonstrating your engagement and desire to understand the content being presented.

Other times in the process, you will contribute as a peer within the group. You will extend their view of what is possible and challenge current assumptions. Here you will assume more of a consultative role. At times, you will have some knowledge of the content; other times you may not. However, in the consultative role, you will need to practice active listening, reflective thinking, and analytical inquiry skills.

Finally, there will be times when the group will clearly need to rely on your expertise and leadership. This is your time to demonstrate why you deserve to be at the table and the value you bring as a leader—not just as a technologist. You want them to value you for more than just the fact that you can make the projector work in the conference room.

Your challenge will be to present your knowledge in ways that expand the understanding of the other group members so they can use the information to make good decisions. In most scenarios, you will likely use skills in areas such as data analysis, project planning, gap analysis, and process modeling. These skills are invaluable regardless of the department in which you work, and effectively demonstrating them builds your credibility as a professional and leader. Selecting the appropriate vocabulary, tone, and style will be critical to your success in this role.

If you gain their trust and confidence in this leadership role, you will have a much easier time when you are assuming other roles in the group. Commit to their success when you are leading, and they will commit to your success when you are not.

Know When to Make the Technology Leap

Most technology leaders assumed that role because they inherently had a fascination with or affinity for technology. That is not a bad thing on its own; however, it does pose a particular challenge—it can lead to the false assumption that everyone shares that same mind-set.

For example, I do not fit the typical CIO profile. I always get a rather shocked reaction when I open a keynote speech by introducing myself and shortly follow up with the statement, "I really dislike technology." You can almost hear the collective gasp ripple through the audience. I usually go on to explain, "I do, however, like what technology allows to occur when it works and is used appropriately." So, I admit it—I am not a gadget freak, and it drives my staff crazy. Yet I feel it has given me a special sensitivity to my customers.

However, since I know many of you have a deeply embedded "techno lust," I feel duty-bound to help. What strategies will you need in place to handle the problem of knowing when to make the technology leap? If we look at the number of emerging technologies dotting the land-scape today, how can we decide which ones are really viable for use in the classroom or office environment? This may very well be one of the most confusing issues you address as the technology leader for your district or organization.

You and the other decision makers are barraged by countless waves of commercial business partners telling you why their solution will make that vital difference to your achievement problem, or save the final penny to balance your budget, or any number of other fantastic claims. Do not get me wrong, private sector partners will be critical to helping reach core missions. However, we must be smart consumers. As a technology leader, your core program goals and objectives must be especially business savvy.

My advice is simple. Ask these questions:

- **How will this improve teaching and learning?**

  This same principle applies even for business or support products and services because they are ultimately supporting the district's core mission. Identify a tangible connection between the proposed product or service and the positive effect on the educational environment.

- **What problem are you trying to solve?**

  Many times people find a technology and then go looking for a problem it can solve. Instead, look at your unmet needs, prioritize them, and then find the best technology to address them. That will help you eliminate many new technologies that may be good ideas but are not something you need now.

- **Is the result worth the effort?**

  Now go back to the section on defining results, and look at what results you are really trying to achieve. It is important to define them in terms that are specific and measurable. Remember, results are the measure of success—not the implementation of a new product or service (the *why* or *so what* factor). If the final result is not worth the level of effort and number of resources it will take to implement the idea, then reconsider your strategy.

- **Can you afford it?**

  This is not actually about money at all. Organizations can usually find the money for the things they really need. However, the costs to implement something new are always much higher than people initially understand.

Identify what organizational capital will be required to implement this technology successfully. Organizational capital can be categorized as fiscal, political, emotional, and productivity-related. Also analyze whether the organization has the resource bandwidth to take on the full scope of support required. These support mechanisms include technical, classroom, or office staff; curriculum integration or work flow; and professional development.

You must have clear guidelines for why and when to integrate technology. The lure of the technology alone cannot be the driving factor. Without guidelines, how will you answer when executives and board members ask, "Why don't the teachers use such and such?"

Living on the Bleeding Edge

Inevitably, technology leaders are faced with the dreaded question about whether an emerging technology should be introduced into their organizations. Bleeding edge, cutting edge, or mainstream: Technology should never be the driver. The instructional or business need must always be the reason for adopting a new product or service, and the intended results should be clearly identified as likely to have a significant positive effect on the educational environment. There are some unique aspects to this emerging technology issue that must be examined separately, given the rapid rate of change associated with technology.

Public education, by nature, is an institution whose reaction to change is based on evolution, not revolution. As a result, it has great difficulty accepting radical shifts in culture, processes, or tools. Schools often find themselves struggling to manage the problems that technology has created. For example, instant messaging, cell phones, MP3s, chat rooms, and blogs have pushed the boundaries of policy and culture for many school districts. The reaction has spanned the continuum from excessively restrictive to naively permissive.

Clearly, as a technology leader, you already find yourself in the middle of this debate, and you are asked to provide leadership in terms of developing and implementing district policy. However, the key to developing practical and effective policies lies in your ability to stay informed about a rapidly changing technology environment, statutory challenges and updates, and evolving best practices. You must also be politically sensitive to the local community's expectations and its members' readiness to accept change.

Finally, you must be able to look at how technology changes or how new policies impact the instructional program within your district. Many of these new tools can make valuable contributions in a classroom, as well as disruptive ones. The key to shifting the balance is technical and instructional preparation, proper training for the teachers and administrators, and practical, enforceable policies and procedures.

Sensei's Advice

- **Always pilot.** When you are going into something new that is a dramatic change, you need to understand its implications before you adopt it as a district standard. However, it is also important to have a structured evaluation methodology defined *before* you begin the project. This includes defining what conditions must be met before the pilot will be expanded. The evaluation keeps pilots from expanding magically without anyone knowing why.

- **Always have a project charter.** Develop a project charter process that outlines the key success factors, evaluation process, support roles and responsibilities, budget and funding sources, and total cost of ownership, and get all key stakeholder departments to sign off on the charter—not just IT. It makes life a lot easier at the end of the project.

Again, this systemic approach will take a great deal of cooperation and collaboration among the IT, staff development, and instructional services departments. It is definitely possible to introduce emerging technologies into your school environment in a positive way. They can extend the learning experience for students into powerful new dimensions, but it takes careful organizational planning and coordination. It also takes skillful management of the political and cultural environment. Finally, it takes teachers who know how to manage the relationships within their classroom to ensure students use the resources appropriately and productively. In the end, it is not about the technology—it is about the learning.

Power Questions

- Are you at the table now for the educational change process? Why or why not? What can you do to change that?

- What skills do you have that can get you to the table?

- Identify a time when you "leaped before you looked" technologically. What would you have done differently?

- What was the last bleeding edge technology your district adopted? Why was it selected? What were the results of the implementation?

The Value of the Teachable Moment

As a technology leader, you understand that one of your goals is to provide solutions that are stable and reliable; the difference between having systems up most of the time versus all of the time can determine successful adoption at the classroom level.

For teachers, the value of each minute of instruction is like gold, to be guarded jealously. Numerous distractions are already built into the school day, such as announcements, assemblies, lunch, and recess.

Still, teachers must ensure that every child reaches the high standards set by their community and legislative officials. The pressure they feel is unlike any generation of teachers before them.

When we as technology leaders go to teachers and say, "We want you to use technology as a part of your instructional practice," there is almost always resistance. This resistance is often based on their personal experiences of poor technology support and instability in technologies they have tried to use in their classroom.

There is nothing worse than building a lesson around a technology component, only to have it fail. That instructional time is lost, and often the attention and focus of the students is lost as well. True, skilled teachers know how to roll with the flow. However, for novice educators and those already timid about technology, this type of experience is a sure death knell for future experiments. These teachers are unlikely to put themselves into this vulnerable position again without significant support from external sources.

- Strive to build a practical level of redundancy into your network infrastructure to reduce single points of failure. Each school district will have to decide to what degree it can afford to implement this practice; however, no district can afford to ignore it totally. The key is minimizing possible points of failure in critical system areas.

- Look at your service-level support contracts for key technology components (critical application servers, communication systems, routers, and so on). Determine what downtime and response time are acceptable to your user community. Engage the senior-level decision makers of the school district in this cost-benefit discussion so they understand what the trade-offs are for longer versus shorter response times.

- Implement monitoring and management tools to determine whether your network bandwidth is sufficient for organizational needs. Teachers will not spend valuable class time waiting for long Internet downloads or slow network response times. You must know what your peak time loads are and what type of traffic is actually moving across those lines. Is it legitimate traffic or stuff that should not be there (e.g., MP3s, streaming videos, large file downloads, and so on)?

▪ Develop, communicate, and deliver practical service-level agreements with your customers for resolving their technical support requests. There is nothing worse than reporting a problem only to hear nothing back, potentially producing the feeling as if the request has disappeared into a black hole. For districts with a small support staff, this may mean outsourcing the repair or support work. The response to support requests must be rapid and predictable. Teachers' equipment has to work—consistently.

Power Questions

▪ Would the majority of your building-level instructional staff consider your technology system to be reliable and stable? What about their classroom resources? Is the trend improving?

▪ How would the building-level instructional staff respond to the adequacy of "just in time" technical support? Is the trend improving?

▪ What are your current service level expectations for your staff? Do these match your customers' expectations? What can be done to bring them closer together?

▪ Where are the "black holes" in your current support operations?

practical activities

This section may be harder for those of you who do not see yourselves as instructional leaders. You may think, "I am not sure I am the right person to lead this discussion or move this agenda forward." You may be partially correct. Trying to do this in isolation would clearly be the wrong tactic. These activities are most effective when done in partnership with the instructional leadership of your district, so see if you can get them to participate.

I realize that in some cases your overture may not be welcomed with open arms. Hopefully, the design of the following activities is such that they will provide enough intrinsic value that your district's instructional leadership will find benefit in them. At the very least, the activities can lead to spirited discussions within your district that may not have occurred in the past.

Activity 5 ■ Student Artifact Analysis Method (SAAM) of Assessment

Using Student Work to Measure Student Learning and Technology Competency

The worksheets for Activity 5 highlight several key roles that students must master to be successful as knowledge-age workers.

The goal is to get districts looking at the actual work students do to understand whether technology is being incorporated meaningfully and significantly. Merely having well-articulated technology standards in the district is insufficient if it is not reflected in the actual work done by the students.

This activity has three objectives:

1. To increase awareness of the connection between learning outcomes and technology competencies and the need for a broader perspective on cultivating student technology skill development

2. To have the small groups identify characteristics or indicators that support identifying student mastery levels: *emerging, proficient*, or *exemplary*

3. To identify what potential learning opportunity gaps may exist within the context of the types of classroom activities currently occurring

Instructions

1. This activity should begin by organizing participants into a cluster of small groups, where each small group has a broad cross-section of actual samples of student work (artifacts) in which technology was an integral part. This collection should reflect the scope of work students are typically exposed to throughout the course of a grading term.

2. Using Activity 5—Worksheet 1, the group should examine each sample to determine what *roles* and *learning outcomes* are best represented by the work and to what *degree of mastery* they are demonstrated.

3. In some work samples, not all roles will be reflected or appropriate, so the group should simply mark "N/A" (not applicable).

4. After they have finished assessing the student work samples, each small group should discuss what characteristics or indicators helped them determine how they assessed the level of mastery. They should record these indicators on Activity 5—Worksheets 2A–2F.

> **Note.** *Some groups may prefer to do this part of the activity as they go through the process instead of at the end, and others may want to do it before they actually begin. It does not matter when it occurs.*

5. Once these characteristics are identified, be sure to collect them for further use. This is a good time to share with the group that their observations will serve as the foundation for creating performance rubrics for evaluation of future student work.

6. Use another blank Activity 5—Worksheet 1 for this step. Have each small group color code the matrix to show how often students participated in activities that allowed them to build mastery. They will color code the student role and objectives where the student samples showed *complete gaps* (red), *low frequency* (yellow), and *high frequency* (green).

7. Have each small group share their findings on the gap analysis with the large group to see what type of correlation there was among the groups.

This material is adapted from the student technology standards of and used with the permission of the Kent School District, Kent, WA.

ACTIVITY 5 ▪ WORKSHEET 1

Student Artifact Analysis Method (SAAM) of Assessment

This worksheet helps put student learning and technology use into a meaningful context.

Instructions

Use the matrix to evaluate student work for evidence of meeting technology competencies in terms of learning outcomes. Check the degree to which the student work supports the learning outcome in the appropriate column for each student role.

		DEGREE EVIDENCED				
Student Role	**Learning Outcome**	1	2	3	4	5
Information navigator	Uses online and electronic resources to communicate, collaborate, and retrieve information in a way that supports learning and personal productivity.					
Critical thinker and analyzer	Researches and evaluates the accuracy, relevance, appropriateness, comprehensiveness, and bias of electronic information sources concerning real-world problems.					

Degree Evidenced Key:
1 = None   **2** = Emerging   **3** = Proficient   **4** = Exemplary   **5** = N/A

Student Role	Learning Outcome	DEGREE EVIDENCED				
		1	2	3	4	5
Creator of knowledge	Uses a variety of technology resources and applications to facilitate learning throughout the curriculum and supports personal, academic, and professional productivity.					
Effective communicator	Designs, develops, publishes, and presents multimedia or online products and presentations using technology resources that demonstrate and communicate curriculum concepts to audiences inside and outside the classroom.					
Technician	Understands and communicates using accurate terminology, common uses of technology in daily life, and understands the advantages and disadvantages those uses provide.					
Ethical user	Advocates and applies positive social and ethical behaviors when using technology and understands the consequences of misuse as a responsible citizen, worker, learner, community member, and family member in a technological age.					

Degree Evidenced Key:
1 = None   **2** = Emerging   **3** = Proficient   **4** = Exemplary   **5** = N/A

ACTIVITY 5 ■ WORKSHEET 2A

Indicators of Mastery: Information Navigator

Identify the *characteristics* and *indicators* that would cause a student's work to be rated as: emerging, proficient, and exemplary. Complete this list for all skill levels within each student role. Be sure to use the learning outcome as the baseline for defining the key characteristics and indicators for that role.

Characteristics are defined as what general learning outcomes related to this role you would expect to see in student work.

Indicators are defined as what specific examples in an artifact or work clearly indicated or reinforced evidence of the student's mastery of the learning outcome.

Student Role: Information Navigator		
Uses online and electronic resources to communicate, collaborate, and retrieve information in a way that supports his/her learning and personal productivity.		
Skill Level	**Characteristics**	**Indicators**
Emerging		
Proficient		
Exemplary		

ACTIVITY 5 ■ WORKSHEET 2B

Indicators of Mastery:
Critical Thinker and Analyzer

Identify the *characteristics* and *indicators* that would cause a student's work to be rated as: emerging, proficient, and exemplary. Complete this list for all skill levels within each student role. Be sure to use the learning outcome as the baseline for defining the key characteristics and indicators for that role.

Characteristics are defined as what general learning outcomes related to this role you would expect to see in student work.

Indicators are defined as what specific examples in an artifact or work clearly indicated or reinforced evidence of the student's mastery of the learning outcome.

Student Role: Critical Thinker and Analyzer

Researches and evaluates the accuracy, relevance, appropriateness, comprehensiveness, and bias of electronic information sources concerning real-world problems.

Skill Level	Characteristics	Indicators
Emerging		
Proficient		
Exemplary		

ACTIVITY 5 ■ WORKSHEET 2C

Indicators of Mastery: Creator of Knowledge

Identify the *characteristics* and *indicators* that would cause a student's work to be rated as: emerging, proficient, and exemplary. Complete this list for all skill levels within each student role. Be sure to use the learning outcome as the baseline for defining the key characteristics and indicators for that role.

Characteristics are defined as what general learning outcomes related to this role you would expect to see in student work.

Indicators are defined as what specific examples in an artifact or work clearly indicated or reinforced evidence of the student's mastery of the learning outcome.

Student Role: Creator of Knowledge

Uses a variety of technology resources and applications to facilitate learning throughout the curriculum and to support personal, academic, and professional productivity.

Skill Level	Characteristics	Indicators
Emerging		
Proficient		
Exemplary		

ACTIVITY 5 ■ WORKSHEET 2D

Indicators of Mastery: Effective Communicator

Identify the *characteristics* and *indicators* that would cause a student's work to be rated as: emerging, proficient, and exemplary. Complete this list for all skill levels within each student role. Be sure to use the learning outcome as the baseline for defining the key characteristics and indicators for that role.

Characteristics are defined as what general learning outcomes related to this role you would expect to see in student work.

Indicators are defined as what specific examples in an artifact or work clearly indicated or reinforced evidence of the student's mastery of the learning outcome.

Student Role: Effective Communicator

Designs, develops, publishes, and presents multimedia or online products and presentations using technology resources that demonstrate and communicate curriculum concepts to audiences inside and outside the classroom.

Skill Level	Characteristics	Indicators
Emerging		
Proficient		
Exemplary		

ACTIVITY 5　■　WORKSHEET 2E

Indicators of Mastery: Technician

Identify the *characteristics* and *indicators* that would cause a student's work to be rated as: emerging, proficient, and exemplary. Complete this list for all skill levels within each student role. Be sure to use the learning outcome as the baseline for defining the key characteristics and indicators for that role.

Characteristics are defined as what general learning outcomes related to this role you would expect to see in student work.

Indicators are defined as what specific examples in an artifact or work clearly indicated or reinforced evidence of the student's mastery of the learning outcome.

Student Role: Technician

Understands and communicates using accurate terminology and common uses of technology in daily life and understands the advantages and disadvantages those uses provide.

Skill Level	Characteristics	Indicators
Emerging		
Proficient		
Exemplary		

ACTIVITY 5 ■ WORKSHEET 2F

Indicators of Mastery: Ethical User

Identify the *characteristics* and *indicators* that would cause a student's work to be rated as: emerging, proficient, and exemplary. Complete this list for all skill levels within each student role. Be sure to use the learning outcome as the baseline for defining the key characteristics and indicators for that role.

Characteristics are defined as what general learning outcomes related to this role you would expect to see in student work.

Indicators are defined as what specific examples in an artifact or work clearly indicated or reinforced evidence of the student's mastery of the learning outcome.

Student Role: Ethical User

Advocates and applies positive social and ethical behaviors when using technology. Understands the consequences of misuse as a responsible citizen, worker, learner, community member, and family member in a technological age.

Skill Level	Characteristics	Indicators
Emerging		
Proficient		
Exemplary		

Activity 6 ■ **Shaping Goals for Results**

In the previous chapter, we talked at length about the importance of aligning the IT department's vision with the broader vision of the district. In this chapter, we spent most of our time discussing the pivotal role the IT department must play in using instruction as a filter for shaping the activities and strategic direction of the department. We also talked at length about how you as the leader must assume a very visible presence in that discussion regardless of the background you bring to the organization.

In this exercise, you will begin to see how you can use this knowledge to shape and drive your goal-setting process in terms that may be very different from what you are accustomed to. In this activity, you will focus on developing a goal-setting process around a results-oriented approach with a strong focus on instruction. Activity 6—Worksheet 1 outlines key areas for you to consider as you identify your department goals—areas that force you to go beyond a project, process, or service delivery model.

This introspection may feel uncomfortable at first, and it may cause some leaders to stretch themselves and their teams into new directions. I encourage you to take the risk and push through—the end result will be worth the effort. You will find that your team's work will be more meaningful for them professionally. Additionally, your district will be able to recognize the value of your department more readily. You can show them that IT is not an endless black hole that simply drains resources!

Instructions

1. Assemble your IT leadership team or your IT staff (depending on the size of your district) and distribute a copy of Activity 6—Worksheet 1. If your relationship is such that you can bring in department representatives from outside IT, this exercise will be even more powerful.

2. Begin your discussion by reflecting on the IT goals currently in place. Use the worksheet to evaluate them on the various characteristics. You are looking for trends and gaps. This is not an exercise that implies you are doing everything wrong, but rather, one that identifies where you can improve.

3. Now that you have identified the key gaps or trends, discuss which ones should be addressed first. The best filters to use for this discussion are:

    ■ What will have the greatest effect on creating a student-centered learning environment?

    ■ What will help us move toward a *results-oriented* environment?

    ■ What will move us toward achieving the vision faster or more effectively?

4. Then have your team look at the existing goals to strengthen them in order to reach the desired outcomes. Make sure the group uses the worksheet to increase the likelihood of success.

5. Next have your team identify what new goals would be needed to help your district achieve these outcomes. The key here is getting the ideas on paper without pre-judging them. Focus on good brainstorming strategies that allow you to collect ideas rapidly (some are covered in chapter 5).

6. Once the ideas are out, begin evaluating them using the worksheet. It provides a neutral way to evaluate their viability without regard for who offered the ideas. You should look for the ideas with the highest impact. As a department, you should not implement or take on too many new goals—no matter how good they are.

7. Finally, garner consensus from the group once you have identified the collection of goals targeted for implementation. This shared ownership is critical, especially during the later stages of implementation and during periods of potential conflict.

The political aspect of organizational leadership is often one of the most difficult for technology leaders to navigate successfully. As a result, it can cause even the best programs to flounder. This group-oriented process can help minimize the risk.

ACTIVITY 6 ■ WORKSHEET 1

Shaping Goals for Results

Success is not whether the innovation itself has been implemented but what has actually happened for students. Carl Glickman believes that the *"litmus test for a good school is not its innovations but rather the solid, purposeful, enduring results it tries to obtain for its students."* (Schmoker, 1996)

Goal _____

How do you rate your goal for success? Is it...	1 = Strongly Disagree 10 = Strongly Agree
Focused on making a difference for learners?	1 2 3 4 5 6 7 8 9 10
Comments:	
Designed to align with the vision?	1 2 3 4 5 6 7 8 9 10
Comments:	
Chosen for generating visible results?	1 2 3 4 5 6 7 8 9 10
Comments:	
Jointly owned by appropriate stakeholders?	1 2 3 4 5 6 7 8 9 10
Comments:	

Perceived as worth doing?	1 2 3 4 5 6 7 8 9 10
Comments:	

Determined as doable?	1 2 3 4 5 6 7 8 9 10
Comments:	

Capable of being measured?	1 2 3 4 5 6 7 8 9 10
Comments:	

Launched with baseline data?	1 2 3 4 5 6 7 8 9 10
Comments:	

In tune with the political realities of the district?	1 2 3 4 5 6 7 8 9 10
Comments:	

This tool is based on work from Bernajean Porter's Grappling with Accountability: Resource Tools for Organizing and Assessing Technology for Student Results and is used with the author's permission.

chapter 5

what makes
a great team?

If you want to go fast,
then go alone;
If you want to go far,
then go together.

African proverb

Max's Journey

"Today has been one of those days that make you wonder why you bothered to get out of bed," thought Max as he arrived on campus for his class. The district's primary router decided to die right in the middle of the school day. The customer support center was flooded with calls by irate teachers as they lost all Internet connectivity. On a different battlefront, his team ran into yet another obstacle in the wireless deployment. Max was about ready to abandon the project and instead issue paper cups and fishing lines. Now, to top it off, he was going to attend his first session with Professor Oracle. The subject was team building. He could only imagine what that was going to be like.

Max entered the classroom. His anxiety increased as the time for class to begin drew near and the number of students enrolled appeared very small. Finally, Professor Oracle glided into the classroom, once again dressed in earth-tone garb with a large tangle of beads around her neck.

The professor put a woven-grass tote bag on the desk and, removing a class roster, moved among the students. She began calling names. As she did so, she would shake the hand of each student and ask them a couple questions about their background and interests before moving on. Max thought this was unusual, but it was an interesting approach for getting to know the class.

After meeting all the students in the class, Professor Oracle asked them to rearrange the desks in a circle. She took her place within the circle and began.

"Team building. Don't worry—we're not going to hold hands and sing 'Kumbaya'. But it is important for your team or staff to have a strong sense of community. However, cohesion is best accomplished through effective hiring practices and managing staff to high levels of performance. 'Touchy-feely' exercises are not required; in fact, they will usually seem contrived and even counterproductive in the absence of effective management.

"So instead, we will spend the majority of our time exploring how to build high-performing teams. This class will follow the key stages of team building and your role in developing and empowering teams.

"When each team member feels individually accountable for the success of every other team member, that's when you truly have a great team. Otherwise, you merely have a group of people working together, which may or may not be a good thing.

"In order to maximize your efforts to build an effective team, you need to understand several key human resource concepts: the developmental stages of teams, conflict resolution principles, interest-based negotiations, and delegation strategies. These best practices can help you significantly elevate the quality of your team and, ultimately, their level of job satisfaction."

Surprised by the professor's depth of knowledge and organized presentation, Max began to relax and focus on what she was saying with renewed respect and interest.

Theory

As Professor Oracle described, when many of us think of team building, we conjure up painful memories of group activities that we found pointless and sometimes embarrassing. This response is quite common and unfortunate. Those well-meaning but misguided efforts in team building are grounded in a lack of understanding of what team building is about. There's a lack of sensitivity to the developmental needs of adults and a fundamental misapplication of core processes.

I do not think the intent behind the touchy-feely activities is anything other than a sincere attempt to improve a team's ability to function well and to improve the overall climate and culture. Yet, the final outcome is often neutral at best, and many times the activities actually have a somewhat negative effect. These results reveal that leaders must clearly understand the theories behind a concept or practice before attempting to use it. That is why I spend time in each chapter covering the background principles and theory before moving on to the application section.

In the next section, we will cover a few basic human resources principles that must be understood in order to build effective teams. These topics include the *developmental stages of teams, delegation strategies,* and *interest-based negotiations.*

Developmental Stages of Teams

Sociologists define groups as a collection of individuals that come together voluntarily, out of necessity, by direction, or through coercion for a common purpose. In 1965, Bruce W. Tuckman from Princeton published his now classic "Forming–Storming–Norming–Performing" model, which describes the developmental nature of small-group dynamics. He indicated that all groups go through a predictable series of developmental stages: *forming, storming, norming,* and *performing.* Tuckman's theory is an elegant and time-tested explanation of team development and behavior.

The following passage, based on my personal experience, is my interpretation and basic use of Tuckman's model.

Forming is the "honeymoon stage," where individuals in the group are on their best behavior. They get along well and generally will not disagree with anything proposed. The discussion or activities really do not go beyond superficial issues. The length of time this period lasts will vary from group to group. Factors such as how often the group meets, how many strong personalities are in the group, or what deadlines the group is under will impact the length of this phase. This is a comfortable stage for a group to be in, but it is not very productive.

Storming is the rocky period that groups often recall much later in the lifespan of the group. This period is either discussed fondly over drinks, or it can linger as bitter gossip in small cliques and poison the culture of your team for months or years to come. Therefore, although it is important to let the team go through this stage, it is equally important to assist them in moving through it as quickly as is practical.

During this period, it is critical to identify the assumptions, biases, prejudices, misconceptions, passions, and agendas team members have brought with them. Once they have been named, it is much easier to develop strategies to handle them in a productive way. If they are left to fester silently, they will poison the team-building process continually in many overt or covert ways.

Norming is the stage when the team begins to set the guidelines for what it means to be a member of the team. They create the group's culture through these parameters. An important part of this process is that the rules are established through consensus, thus creating shared ownership. Sometimes this is a formal process, while other times it is very informal. Regardless, members of the team all come to know the rules and accept them. This process forms the basis for individual accountability. At this point, it is clear that a social structure has formed within the team.

Another important part of this stage is that this is when real work begins to be accomplished. The team has not hit its true potential yet, but it has clearly identified what is necessary to work effectively as a team.

Performing is the sweet spot for teams. Now is when teams finally hit their stride and begin producing work that is high in quality and quantity. They begin working like a well-oiled machine. Team members know the goals they are working toward, the roles of the team members are clearly defined, and the culture of the team allows for authentic dialogue about how to carry out the task. This level of communication includes the ability to challenge ideas respectfully to get the best possible solutions.

The team knows how to leverage the strengths of individual members and compensate for members' weaknesses. They truly share responsibility for the team's goals and projects, and they celebrate successes as a team. They enjoy working together, and there is a high level of energy when they do so.

Unfortunately, few teams get to this stage for reasons that include power struggles, personality clashes, lack of goal definition or shared purpose, or poor leadership.

As the leader, it is important to assist the team in moving through the early stages as quickly as possible. Your goal is to get your team to the *performing* stage. However, they cannot skip the earlier stages. If they do, they will be merely a group of people with reduced effectiveness as they hit problems later. So although it may be frustrating to have people go through the full cycle, it is important from a developmental perspective to strengthen the team dynamics.

Delegation Strategies

One of the least-understood areas of leadership is delegation. Most leaders know delegation is a critical skill to develop and must be used to survive; however, they were never really taught how to do it effectively. Delegation is essential, though, in developing strong teams. It is a clear indicator to your staff that you value and trust their ability to get things done. It shows them you do not always need to be in charge and that you are not the only one capable of providing leadership within the department. Demonstrating these principles is important for your long-term success.

What are the rules for when to delegate and when to hold on to control for dear life? There are no hard and fast rules, but I have found a few practical guidelines that are useful in making that decision.

When is it safe to delegate project leadership responsibility?

- When the risk level is low

- When the scope and cost of the project are low

- When the deadline is relaxed or distant

- When the project is clearly defined with measurable outcomes

- When the expertise and experience base of the proposed leader is high

- When you have built in multiple safeguards and monitoring mechanisms

Any one of these guidelines, by itself, may not be enough to make a project a prime candidate for delegation; however, if the project has several of these characteristics then it clearly becomes a good possible target.

Other factors to consider are the following:

- What are the political implications associated with the project?

- Who are the affected stakeholders?

- How long have you been in your position?

Yes, some of these would be subsets of the indicators mentioned previously. However, I think they are important enough to pull them out for special consideration. Clearly, they have higher potential for negative fallout, and, therefore, you need to consider them separately regardless of the other factors. That does not mean you should not delegate, but it may require you to build in extra monitoring mechanisms so you know more about what is going on.

Interest-Based Negotiations

Interested-based negotiations or discussions are a common practice in the field of human resources and labor relations, especially in contract deliberations. This strategy is often used to bring parties together when there is conflict over settling a dispute or reaching an agreement during contract negotiations.

The concept was originally proposed by Roger Fisher in 1981. The concept requires the opposing parties to begin by focusing on what common interests they share and place them on the table as agreements. Identifying the common ground the parties share makes it easier to discuss the areas where they are not aligned. Interests define the problem, but how do you identify interests? Ask "Why?" Ask "Why Not?" Think about their choice. Interest-based negotiations also help to bolster the relationship in a positive way and diffuse some of the negative energy that may exist between the parties. This approach is a powerful technique for resolving conflicts within teams and between individuals.

Conclusion

With this background knowledge of the developmental nature of teams, delegation strategies and criteria, and interest-based negotiation, you have powerful tools to strengthen your team-building skills. These human resources strategies can help you focus on each individual's needs in your department or team. You will learn how to bring individuals together to resolve conflicts, focus on common goals, and build their leadership capacities. The end result will be a stronger core department capable of assisting you in reaching your vision.

Power Questions

- What stage would you say your department as a whole is in today? How long has it been there? What is keeping it there?

- Do you have any teams within your department that are at the *performing* stage? How can they help other teams in your department that are not at the *performing* stage?

- Do you have any teams in the *storming* stage? What specific actions are you taking to help them move to the next stage?

- What criteria do you use today to determine how and when you delegate a decision or project? Is your team aware of this criteria? What is their criteria?

- When was the last time you could have used interest-based negotiation to turn a negative situation to a positive one? How could this process supplement your conflict resolution strategies?

Application

We've learned that all teams go through a developmental cycle. Now we need to explore what our role is as a leader at each stage in this cycle. We will begin the section by discussing how you can provide leadership to teams working within your department. The primary focus is not managing the department-wide team, but rather, managing project-based teams, which are formed on an on-going basis.

Some teams are comprised entirely of IT staff, while others integrate staff from other departments. Look at this possible combining of departments as an opportunity to provide a level of leadership that other leaders may not have the expertise to offer. By understanding the developmental nature of teams, you can be a valuable resource as they move through the various developmental stages. It is a great way to build bridges to other departments and demonstrate your own value.

Remember, as leaders we are usually action focused, and as a result, we have a natural tendency to want to push the group through the developmental stages of teaming quickly. You may even think about skipping certain stages in order to get the team to the desired stage of performing. After all, that is where the real work can occur. Remember my earlier caution, though—if your team skips a stage, you will pay for it in the long run. The team will be less capable of handling conflict and problem solving in positive and appropriate ways. Your real goal is to have a team, not just a group of people working together.

So, what should you be doing as you lead teams in the various stages of Tuckman's model?

Forming

Here the group will be in the feel-good stage, and there will generally be minimal conflict. However, they will also tend to avoid the project's tough issues. Often this stage involves a great deal of data gathering and understanding the project's organizational context. Your level of direct involvement is minimal, and during this stage you should be prepared for minimal output from the group. Fortunately, this stage is usually very brief.

Depending on your particular style of leadership, you may want to sit in on the initial team meetings to observe the group dynamics and process flow and to show support for the project or team.

Eventually the honeymoon must end. Group members will start to tackle the tough issues they have avoided. People will try to figure out what roles they are supposed to play within the group and may struggle for more or less responsibility. Members that are normally high performers may become frustrated with those who appear not to be pulling their weight. These problems highlight any lack of formal group processes and structures. Other behaviors start to eat away at the cohesiveness of the group. For example, people start showing up late for meetings or skipping them all together. Often they will come unprepared or without completing their assigned tasks.

It is this growing dissonance that causes the weak group processes to break down even further, and the accountability process all but disappears. The frustrations grow significantly in the group, and some members begin to disengage further, while others become more vocal and agitated. The little work that was happening begins to slow down, and only a few individuals seem to be contributing. When these symptoms start to occur, you know that the team has moved into the storming phase.

Sensei's Advice

- Lead or appoint a team leader.

- Understand the purpose of the group and the roles the team members are to play.

- Understand what boundaries the team must operate within and any nonnegotiable guidelines.

- Share all of this information with the group at the beginning to prevent the team from forming any misconceptions about the range of authority or scope of task. It also helps them to understand whether their role is advisory, decision making, or implementation.

- Define the parameters of the task to be accomplished, its timelines, and the resources available.

- Assign a project leader to conduct the project meetings and coordinate team members' activities.

Storming

Once a team reaches this stage, everyone wants to give up and do anything but work on the project. As the leader, you have a vital role to play at this point. Many leaders want to ignore the tensions and tell the team to plow through it to get the work done. Another strategy many leaders often use is to call the group together and tell them to work it out as the leader steps back and walks away from the situation. While these approaches may appear to be efficient and even appropriate for adults who are "professionals," they can ultimately damage your department in ways that could take months or years to overcome.

This stage is to be expected, and it is necessary for a team to reach its full potential. Your role is to help the team work through it in a positive and healthy manner. The most important thing you can achieve is to preserve self-respect for all individuals within the team, while not allowing the work to grind to a complete halt.

Of course, your personal leadership style comes into consideration. You can step up and take a very direct role in

Sensei's Advice

- Decide whether to intervene directly or coach the team leader.

- Solve the right problem. It is important not to get wrapped up in the symptoms. You will need to identify the root causes of problems.

- Identify what group processes are missing or not working and help build them.

- Provide group members with new ways to communicate their frustrations and strategies for resolving their differences with each other.

- Monitor, monitor, monitor. Watch team members very carefully to see whether they are progressing though this stage, and watch for changes in behaviors.

managing the team dynamics and conflict resolution process. Or, you might choose to work with the project leader and coach him or her on strategies to move the team forward positively.

The following are important criteria that can help you decide when to step in versus delegate. You should not delegate the leadership role when:

- the project is high-risk or high-profile for the department or organization,

- the project leader is leading a group for the first time on a team with more experienced team leaders,

- the project leader is in charge of a team where he or she is outranked by senior members in the organization,

- the project was not launched well or failed previously, or

- you are new to the organization—you should probably intervene more often.

Remember, this stage is normally a period of conflict and stress for the team, so expect minimal output and success. They do not like being in this stage any more than you like them being there.

Sometimes conflict within a team grows out of a misunderstanding of the scope of the project's outcomes. This lack of clarity allows each team member to develop his or her own vision for where the project is headed, and each one acts based on those assumptions. When a team member does something that does not fit within another team member's frame of reference, conflict can ensue.

This lack of agreement on the project's direction can be a significant and disastrous source of dissonance for any team. As the leader, either directly or indirectly, you need to help the team understand where it is going and dispel misconceptions about its tasks. The best way to do that is to help them define what is within the scope of their project and what is outside of the scope. You also need to help them understand their roles and functions.

Even a veteran technology leader may need a few new strategies to move the group through this troubled phase. I have found the interest-based discussions technique, described above, to be quite effective. A closer look at interest-based discussions is provided in the following section.

Interest-Based Discussions

Because team members may have conflicts on any number of issues, one of the most powerful strategies is to get them to agree on something. Using the interest-based discussions or negotiations technique to work through their issues can be very helpful. So, how would you implement the interest-based discussions or negotiations technique within a group setting?

1. On a pad of large chart paper, identify what key project concepts, procedures, and principles all group members support. Post them clearly so the group can easily see the list. You can regularly refer back to the points of agreement when conflicts occur. This is a great way to diffuse the negative energy in a room.

2. Now that you have collected the significant points of agreement or shared interests, the next step is to make sure all group members understand and agree on the final outcomes. Begin by having the group restate the desired outcomes. Record them on the chart paper so the entire group can see them. As you get a specific outcome posted, begin asking individuals to describe what that outcome means to them. Have them get very specific about it. When individuals are asked to be definitive, they will reveal any assumptions or misconceptions associated with their knowledge of the outcome.

3. Ask others in the group whether they understand the outcome in the same way. If they all agree, move on to the next one.

If they do not agree, ask someone to explain how he or she views it differently. Be sure to record what was specifically different about this view of the outcome. Poll the group again, asking if that was how they understood it. Be sure to allow time for everyone to ask clarifying questions until they all understand the outcome.

> ## What is a clarifying question?
>
> A clarifying question is designed to expand an individual's understanding of a concept; however, it is not allowed to challenge or attempt to change the group's point of view. The goal is to provide everyone in a group the level of understanding necessary to permit them to support the group's direction or decision.

If the group still does not agree, then ask another person to identify his or her perspective. Continue this process until you have identified all of the varied ideas. You should see duplications very soon. At that point, ask whether someone has an interpretation that is different from what is already recorded. If so, add it to the charts. Once you have clearly identified the team's outcomes and gained a unified understanding from the group, you are ready to move to the next stage.

4. Now you can tackle any disconnection that remains within the team. At this point you should find that some of the disagreements that existed when the team came into the room will have already disappeared as a result of each individual's new level of understanding. However, there will still be important issues to tackle.

First, poll the group to identify what concerns they have about reaching the outcomes. The terminology you choose can set the tone, so be thoughtful in how you ask about their concerns.

Terms you might want to use include *gaps, growth challenges, potential obstacles,* and *stretch opportunities.*

5. As you collect the remaining problems, help the group focus on the solutions. The real key is to eliminate the concern in a way that moves the team forward toward achieving its identified outcomes. Then, whatever the issue is becomes less about any person or group and more about achieving the outcome, which is a shared interest for the team.

   Another tip is to help the team identify multiple solutions for each gap. Then they can explore the advantages and disadvantages of the various solutions in terms of which one will move them closer to achieving their outcome. This strategy will move them away from the emotion of the original conflict.

Remember, the sooner the team becomes a problem-solving machine, focused on its end goal, the faster it will catapult to the next stage: norming. Once the team is near the end of the storming phase, you can introduce the concept of group operating norms, so members begin thinking about how they want to operate as a group. Many of the norms will be generated from the discussion that has already occurred.

Norming

Norms are defined as the set of rules or guidelines that the team agrees to operate by. The best norms respect the team, increase group effectiveness, and hold all team members accountable to each other. The leader should ensure that the group works through the norming stage in an inclusive manner.

The following are the schools of thought when it comes to developing group norms:

1. Let the team brainstorm over the list of guidelines, and then spend time discussing the list. Have the team prioritize the list until members come up with a final version they believe

all members can live with. This decision-making process is accomplished by arriving at a consensus, not by voting. Consensus means group members realize, "I may not personally think this is the best idea, but I can live with it. For the good of the group, I agree to abide by it."

2. The leader brings a proposal of norms for the group to consider. Members can revise the list, throw it away and come up with their own list, or adopt it in its original form. Again, the final step is achieved through consensus.

The goal is to have all group members agree they will abide by the norms for the good of the group. The norms drive their individual behaviors; the group is responsible for holding each member accountable for the norms. The norms are also the mechanisms that take the group to the next level of cohesiveness, and the byproduct of that is increased productivity.

What types of behaviors should be included in team norms? If we begin with the goals of increasing team effectiveness, respecting the team members, and holding individuals accountable to the team, then we derive several powerful norms for shaping teams.

Sensei's Advice

- Facilitate team members as they develop their group norms, or work with the team leader so that he or she can facilitate the group.

- State the expectation in advance that all group norms must align with the department's values and vision.

- Identify possible accountability options for members to choose from before they begin the development process, unless they choose to create their own.

- Encourage and celebrate their progress. Success breeds more success.

The following behaviors are examples of norms. Team members will:

- arrive at meetings on time and be well prepared;
- listen, actively seeking to understand, before speaking;
- challenge the concept while respecting the person presenting it;
- actively engage in the meeting, avoiding external distractions;
- present facts first and then opinions;
- maintain the group's confidentiality; and
- focus on solutions and minimize dwelling on obstacles.

The norming stage is about more than just identifying these norms—it is also about how the team begins to put these guidelines into practice as they conduct their work. During the next few meetings, they may awkwardly implement them with varying degrees of success. However, as they grow more comfortable with the norms and experience success, you will see the group mature. The culture of the group will begin to evolve as well. When this happens, you see a noticeable shift in group productivity, participation, and climate. They are now moving into the last phase: *performing*.

Performing

As the team moves into the performing stage and begins to function as a cohesive group, you will probably wonder, "What is my role now?" Your natural tendency may be to back off, and in many cases, that is exactly what you should do. But just how far can you back off? My rule of thumb is to stay within the *awareness zone*. What is the awareness zone? It is the distance that allows you to know what is going on and how well it is going, while allowing the group the freedom to function independently.

Why is this independence important? Remember, one of your goals is to continue building the leadership capacity of your team members. They cannot grow as leaders if they feel you are constantly looking over their shoulders. But we also know that, as the leaders, we are still accountable for the final product and any mishaps that occur along the way. Even though the team is working well now, it is always possible for things to regress. That is why the awareness zone is a critical tool for effectively managing teams in the performing stage.

The beauty of having a team in the performing stage is that successes usually generate enough positive energy to keep the team moving forward. The team is producing at high levels and is making real progress toward achieving its final outcomes. It tends to require minimal supervision on your part. That is a good thing, because there are always plenty of other tasks waiting to fill that gap.

An important role you play as the leader during this stage comes at the conclusion of the project. You need to ensure proper closure for the group, which can come in a number of forms:

Sensei's Advice

- Stay out of their way, but stay in the awareness zone.

- Remove any authentic obstacles that get in the way of their progress immediately. Keep them moving forward.

- Encourage and celebrate their progress.

- Create end-of-project evaluation and reflection opportunities.

- Create opportunities for end-of-project celebration.

- Recognize individual contributions to the project's success.

- Conduct a formal or informal debriefing with the team on the positive aspects of being involved with the project, lessons learned from the challenges, what accomplishment they are most proud of in the project, and so on.

- Hold a concluding celebration for the team, where they can share their favorite memories from the project or something they appreciated about particular team members.

- Send a personal note of congratulations and appreciation to each team member for his or her contribution to the project and its successful completion.

The type of activities you choose to do should be appropriate and aligned with your personal leadership style and organizational culture.

Developmental Regression

Now that the team has reached this stage, many leaders breathe a sigh of relief. I hate to break the news to you, but backsliding to a previous stage is possible. What can cause developmental regression? The following are a few possible factors:

- New group members are introduced into the team.

- Key teams or people are removed from the group.

- The timeline for the project is drastically altered.

- The scope of the project is drastically altered.

- The executive sponsor for the project is changed.

When these types of significant changes are made to the team at nearly any point in the development cycle, it will usually cause the team to revert to the forming or storming stage, depending on the scale of the change. Before making a change to a team that is working well, be sure the change is really worth the possible repercussions.

Managing Unsuccessful Teams

Up to now, we have talked about the team in terms of it becoming successful. Unfortunately, as we all know, not all teams make the transition to performing, and ultimately, not all projects conclude successfully.

I have witnessed projects' postmortems when the leader really grills the team on its failures. Yet, I seldom see the leader take any ownership. Leaders usually don't want to identify where they let the team down or admit they could have done better. However, if they would display a realistic level of vulnerability and openness, it would make a world of difference.

As the leader, you are responsible for your team's results regardless of whether the team gets it together or not. They are not in charge; you are. You should begin the postmortem by analyzing your own role in the failure *before* you meet with the team and then be prepared to share your insights.

1. First, you need to step up and own the outcome.

2. Next, take time to reflect on the root causes of the team's failure or the project's failure. Be careful not to focus merely on symptoms.

3. Ask yourself, "What was my role in it?" and "What could I have done differently?"

Gather the team together and be upfront with them about the fact that they did not meet the goal. Mention, as well, that you appreciate the effort they put forth and that your intent is not to cast blame or seek a scapegoat. Rather, you wish to analyze the project so your team can learn how to improve in the future. This is the perfect time for you to share the insights from your personal reflection. It will set the tone for a positive and open conversation.

Ask team members to identify what they believe were the key factors in the project not meeting the identified outcomes. If possible, refer back to the outcomes created during the norming or storming phase. Rather than focusing on a particular person who did not perform well, focus on a key criterion that was not accomplished.

Once the root causes have been identified, have the members brainstorm alternative ways they could have dealt with the problems. Next, have them identify what kept them from choosing those alternative paths. This will help the group determine what "blinders" may prevent them from seeing alternative solutions in future projects. Sample blinders might include the following:

- tight deadlines,

- budget constraints,

- lack of authority,

- lack of understanding,

- technical limitations, and

- just didn't think about it.

Often you will find the same blinders are present from project to project. It is important for your staff to think about ways to overcome these blinders so they can become more effective problem solvers.

Close the session by having the team focus on moving forward positively. Some of them might be working together on other projects. They need to put the failure behind them but not the lessons learned from it.

Now return to your personal reflections from prior to meeting with the team. Compare your initial impressions about the project with the feedback that you gathered from the group. The following are two key questions you might want to ask yourself:

1. Does this alter my perception about my role in the project?

2. What could or should I have done to increase the likelihood of a successful outcome?

The answers are an important gauge of how in touch you were with the team and the dynamics of what was going on. If you delegated your role as leader, it will let you know whether you delegated appropriately. In other words, were you in the awareness zone? Although we never want a team to fail, it is a powerful learning opportunity for them and for you. Be sure to leverage it to its fullest.

Power Questions

- In what group developmental stage is your leadership style most effective? Why? Least effective? Why?

- What was the best team of which you were a part? Why was it so successful? How can you create that type of experience for your staff?

- On average, what percentage of your small-group teams make it to the *performing* stage? If not 100%, why? What are you doing to reach 100%?

- How many of your teams shifted from *performing* back to *forming* or *storming* as a result of changes you instituted? Was the change really necessary? Was the payoff worth it?

- When was the last time you began a postmortem with a team by personally taking ownership of the project's failure? What was the team's reaction? When will you do it next?

The Sensei's Parting Thoughts

- We looked at the development stages that all groups move through: forming, storming, norming, and performing.

- We discussed factors to be considered when deciding whether to delegate decision making and the leadership role.

- We looked at a new strategy for conflict resolution: interest-based negotiation or discussion. The focus is on beginning where the parties have shared interests and moving ahead from there.

- We explored in depth the specific leadership roles you should play as your team moves through the developmental stages.

- We identified potential factors that can cause teams to regress developmentally and the impact this can have on performance.

- We discussed how to help unsuccessful teams conduct positive and productive post-project evaluation sessions.

Clearly, team building is much more than simply getting your staff together to conduct personality surveys and trust-building exercises. Team building is also not only about creating a pleasant work environment, although that is a wonderful by-product of high-performing teams.

What's critical is a broad understanding of what it takes to grow and manage mature, capable teams who can produce at high levels with strong, independent leadership. You also must know what to do when this is not occurring within your department. The leadership skill of authentic, comprehensive team building is critical to achieve success in reaching your goals for the department.

practical activities

Activity 7 ▪ **Project Scoping for Conflict Resolution**

Is your team having difficulty with a project? Do you suspect it may be because of a lack of agreement on the project's scope? This activity is designed to engage and visually reinforce a team so they can get back on the same page with regard to their project. At the completion, the team should have a clearer vision of where they are going and what they can let go of, emotionally and practically.

Instructions

1. Prior to the meeting with the team, draw two large picture frames or just two large rectangles on chart paper.

2. At the beginning of the meeting, hang these two sheets and one or two additional blank sheets of chart paper at the front of the room.

3. Distribute a packet of sticky notes to each team member.

4. Ask each team member to reflect on the project goals and outcomes.

5. Have them record what they think are the specific outcomes for the project.

   Tell them to be as specific as possible and to avoid global statements. You can also have them include specific major project activities they believe are included or critical to the project.

   Tell them to write only one item on each sticky note. They can write as many sticky notes as they want.

6. Have everyone come forward and put all their sticky notes on the blank piece of chart paper at the front of the room.

As they return to their seats, scan the notes and try to group duplicates.

7. Begin by selecting a sticky note and polling the group about the item. Have them decide whether the items are "in scope," "out of scope," or "unsure" for the project.

Encourage them to discuss their point of view about their desired placement. Try to gain consensus, if possible. Remember, as the leader you have the final say because you are ultimately responsible for the project.

8. If the item is "in scope," place it inside the picture frame (rectangle) on the chart paper. If the item is "out of scope," place it outside the frame. If the group is "unsure" put it *on* the frame. You'll return to these items later. You want the group to make as many decisions as possible before you step in.

You will find that this process will go fairly quickly. Overall, the group will probably know the scope of the project. When individuals don't understand specific aspects of the project, it will tend to be different pieces for different people, and the group can quickly resolve the misunderstanding.

Sensei's Advice

If your team seems to have trouble beginning this exercise, one suggestion is to let the group focus on what the project is *not about* first. It is strange, but people seem to be able to eliminate items more quickly than choosing items to include. So if they seem to be spinning their wheels, begin by having them cross off things that are clearly out of scope for the project.

9. Complete the activity, including going back to clarify items on the frame.

10. Compile the findings and distribute them to the group.

This document you create at the end of the meeting will reduce future conflict and confusion as the project moves forward.

Activity 8 ▪ **The Attitude Barometer**

Many factors come into play when building an effective learning organization. There must be clearly defined strategic objectives and metrics for performance. However, in building a data-driven decision-making model, the affective domain of information gathering must also be considered. A successful organization/department should also "feel" healthy besides measuring up.

One activity we use to assist in this process is known as the *Attitude Barometer*. The goal of this activity is to get *anonymous, subjective* data from your employees on a specific topic or issue. It is also a simple way to get broad-based data in a short period of time.

Instructions

1. Prior to the meeting, construct an attitude barometer wall chart by placing your question at the top followed by a number line that ranges from 1 to 5. Figure 5.1 illustrates two examples of the attitude barometer chart. Post it near the entrance/exit door to the room. Also place an empty basket or box near this chart.

2. During the meeting or as they enter the session, distribute color-coded sticky notes to your staff members. The color coding allows you to track responses within sub-groups of your department/organization. If your group is small, this step is not necessary. It is OK to let the group know they are color coded for a purpose, but this is not required.

3. Then pose a specific question that necessitates an affective response. This type of question is one not typically included in quantitative measures for an organization. Examples might include: "*I enjoy my current job assignment.*"; "*I feel my contributions are valued by the department.*"; "*Our current strategic direction is positive and exciting.*"

4. Ask each person to rate his or her response to this question on a scale from 1–5. The rating scale we use is: **1.** Strongly Disagree, **2.** Disagree, **3.** Somewhat Agree, **4.** Agree, **5.** Strongly Agree. Also ask them to write *why* they gave that specific rating regardless of whether it is a high or low rating.

You need to collect data from both ends of the rating spectrum. If it is positive, you want to continue and expand those elements of your program. If it is negative, it allows you to determine if it is something that can and should be corrected. Be sure to tell your staff that you will collect the data, analyze it, and share the findings at an upcoming session with them. This validates their input.

5. As the participants leave, tell them they can either place their sticky notes on the wall chart or they may leave them in the basket next to the chart.

This process allows them to be candid in their response with very low risk. You want their honest feedback, and this choice fosters anonymity. However, some people really want to publicly state their view, so the wall chart allows for that as well.

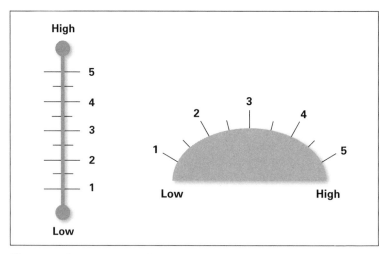

Figure 5.1. Two examples of the attitude barometer wall chart

chapter 6

how am I doing?

Criticism, like rain,
should be gentle enough
to nourish a man's growth
without destroying his roots.

Frank A. Clark,
English football player and coach

Max's Journey

Max could almost see the anxiety emanating from Stan as he silently took the seat opposite Max's desk. Max had been dreading this performance review all day. He knew it would end up frustrating both of them and would probably resolve nothing.

Stan was a total mystery to Max. He joined the IT department about nine months ago, and from the beginning, he struggled to find his niche. Stan was a top-notch technician and clearly knew his stuff. He came with good recommendations from his previous employers, although Max was not sure everyone had been completely forthcoming.

Although Stan's technical skills were excellent, his interpersonal ones needed a lot of work. In meetings he often came across as arrogant. As a result, even though he clearly had a lot to offer and often had the right solution, his team would totally dismiss his input. Consequently, Stan's demeanor became more negative and combative, further escalating the problem.

Max had tried coaching him on appropriate communication strategies. He had shared with Stan methods for presenting ideas in a less confrontational manner. Max had also sent him to a seminar on effective teaming and conflict resolution, hoping this would make a difference. Unfortunately, nothing seemed to cause any lasting change in behavior. On the latest project, the team was practically in revolt. The team leaders had voiced their concerns to Max, basically saying they wanted Stan removed from the project.

Today Max was supposed to conduct Stan's midyear evaluation, and he was struggling to figure out what to say. He really wanted Stan to be successful and believed he could be a valuable part of the IT team. However, unless Stan made major changes in attitude and behavior, Max was going to have to let him go. As Max began the meeting, he thought, "I sure wish I had Professor Sensei with me right now."

Later that evening, Max entered the classroom, feeling drained from the meeting with Stan. Max knew he had been unable to provide the kind of leadership Stan needed. While he was reflecting on this, Professor Sensei walked into the classroom. He smiled as he scanned the class and asked, "How am I doing?" Then he stood there quietly. After several uncomfortable moments of silence, he asked the question again.

One of the students in the front row asked, "What do you mean?"

The professor replied, "I am simply asking you, how am I doing as your instructor? I want your feedback." Then he stood there in silence again.

After a couple of moments, another one of the students in the front row spoke up: "I think you are an excellent instructor."

Professor Sensei continued standing there in silence. Finally, another student responded, "I appreciate the way you try to keep the class interesting."

After several other students responded in similar ways, Max finally spoke up, "Professor, I think you challenge us to dig deeply into ourselves and ask the hard questions. Your insights are keen and valuable to me in my work experience. However, respectfully, I wonder if you are tough enough on us with regard to meeting our deadlines for class projects. After all, as leaders, we must set appropriate expectations and then hold our people accountable for the outcomes. So, the same must be done for us."

A few of students seemed surprised that Max had offered criticism; however, the professor beamed a wide smile at him.

Then Professor Sensei said, "Thank you all for your feedback tonight. Let us continue learning the core strategies of performance management and how they can help you bring out the best in your staff."

Theory

Often when we think of performance management, personnel evaluation comes to mind. We know staff evaluation is a core function of effective supervision. All employees want to know how they are doing and to be assured they are doing a good job.

Unfortunately, the true purpose of staff evaluation is usually lost in the myriad details associated with the process, and, far too often, it becomes merely a "pass/fail" report. This event, only a moment in time, does little to help employees reflect on their personal challenges and successes, understand their contributions to the department's or school's overall success or decline, or set the stage for authentic professional growth and achievement.

Managing Performance: Helping Your Staff Excel

As educators and professionals, we know evaluation is about much more than this snapshot approach. It is also about the progress made during the journey, the final product, and the lessons learned along the way. Those are the bases for current reform efforts in assessment practices across the country. So, why would we not incorporate them into the assessment of our employees' performances?

As leaders, we must take a broader view of managing and evaluating the performance of our staff.

- Leaders must develop leadership capacity in the team and be accountable for the performance of the team.

- Leaders must align expectations for staff performance with the department's or school's vision.

- Leaders must accept the responsibility to help everyone succeed.

In this chapter, we will look at the following key objectives.

Employee Performance Mapping

1. Assess your individual team members and determine how they contribute to the team's culture, performance, and leadership capacity.

2. Use this assessment to understand how different types of individuals can either strengthen or weaken a team as a result of the characteristics they bring within the domains of performance and leadership.

3. Identify what you can do to manage the team's composition, including how to impact the hiring process for new members or transition current members.

Management by Objectives (MBO)

1. Implement performance management principles, including using performance objectives that can help you manage your team's action plans.

2. Use the performance objectives to keep your department aligned with the strategic goals and vision of the school or district.

3. Create a process for understanding how your performance objectives affect the staff evaluation process and how the objectives can be used to drive improvement within your team.

Professional Growth Plans (PGPs)

1. Explore your leadership role in building the capacity of your team to work as independent problem solvers and creative thinkers.

2. Understand and build professional growth plans.

3. Create succession planning to help your team build its individual and collective leadership capacity and efficacy.

These are a few basic human resource principles and practices that will increase your effectiveness in supervision. These concepts will also help you build a more strategic approach to staff assessment. Ironically, more effort to understand this area has been made outside education than inside. Those of you who come from the private sector may already be familiar with many of these ideas.

Employee Performance Mapping

Employee performance mapping, or the four quadrant map, is a very common technique long used in many larger corporations to assist in identifying strengths and areas for improvement during an employee's evaluation conference. Today, it has morphed into something much more involved in many organizations—companies such as GE have turned the technique into a science and use it to manage many aspects of their human resource processes.

The basics of the technique are as follows: each quadrant represents a ranking. All employees on a team are placed within one of four quadrants. Often an individual's performance is ranked relative to the other members of the team. Employee performance mapping is often used to identify who will be targeted for leadership development programs, to identify who will be targeted for downsizing to reduce costs or increase profits, and to determine how annual salary increases are given to employees.

Depending on the philosophy of the organization using this tool, the problem with this approach can be that each year one or more individuals always show up in the lowest-ranking quadrant. It is the very nature of how the instrument is designed. It provides a mechanism continually to exit employees from the team while raising the bar, so team members never feel like they can achieve enough.

If this tool is used appropriately, though, it can be a powerful mechanism for building the capacity of your team. It can help you identify potential problem areas so you can build strategies proactively to resolve them. It will allow you to identify your leaders, so you can leverage them to increase their potential. You can also identify your low performers, so you can determine how you want to cope with them. However, it does not necessarily require you constantly to rank people from top to bottom. With proper coaching and professional development, it is possible to move all team members into the productive quadrants. We will talk more about this at length later in this chapter.

Management by Objectives (MBO)

The Management by Objective (MBO) process has been in use for more than 25 years in the private sector and is a key component in the Total Quality Management (TQM) movement. Total Quality Control was the key concept of Armand Feigenbaum's 1951 book, *Quality Control: Principles, Practice, and Administration*. In a chapter titled "Total Quality Control," Feigenbaum introduced an idea that created a groundswell of interest in the following decades, which would later transform from Total Quality Control to Total Quality Management. W. Edwards Deming, Joseph Juran, Philip B. Crosby, and Kaoru Ishikawa were also key contributors to the body of knowledge now known as TQM. The MBO process assumes that performance objectives drive action plans for organizations. The objectives are tightly aligned with the strategic goals and vision of the department or organization, and it is this alignment that makes them a powerful agent for positive change.

The MBO process is the next logical step from earlier chapters, where we discussed visions and goal setting. Performance objectives are how you take those more abstract concepts and make them concrete and actionable. Ultimately, an ideal MBO implementation is driven all the way down through your organization or department to the individual employee. As a result, every employee has a specific set of performance objectives that are tightly aligned to the performance objectives of the leadership or department. This alignment continues as you move up through the organization.

When there is strong alignment, the results will further the core mission of the organization. Later in this chapter, we will discuss how to create effective performance objectives and turn them into action plans.

Professional Growth Plans (PGPs)

Another key component of the assessment or evaluation process is the development and maintenance of professional growth plans (PGPs). This concept is relatively new to both the private and public sectors. These should not be confused with professional improvement plans (PIPs), which are typically used for struggling employees. The goal in the PGP process is to help the employee, whether he or she is a strong or struggling employee, identify a long-term plan for professional growth and development.

A PGP will include the following components:

- short- and long-term career goals,

- new skills and competencies he or she wishes to develop,

- specific strategies and support mechanisms for acquiring the new skills, and

- other factors that will add additional value to the organization and the individual's professional growth.

A well-developed, focused, professional growth program is mutually beneficial for the employee and the organization. We will spend significant time later in this chapter looking at how to approach this topic differently for your rising and falling stars. We will also discuss its role in employee retention.

Power Questions

- How pleased were you with the quality of *your* last evaluation by your supervisor? What part of it was the most effective? What part of it was the least effective?

- How would your direct reports answer these same questions?

- How much time do you typically take to prepare the evaluations for your staff? How much time do you take in reviewing the progress toward the goals you established for them during the course of the year? What relationship is there between what they do daily and the goals set for them in the evaluation?

- How do you assess the composition of your team with regard to strengths and weaknesses? What do you do with the data? How often do you review the data for changes?

- What are the ways you manage the professional growth of your staff? How is it tied to the evaluation process? How is it tied to their daily action plans?

Application

Every team has a personality or culture. As the leader, you have a dramatic impact on it and can serve as a powerful catalyst to change it—for better or worse. To manage the performance of your team, you must understand the composition of the players within it. They all bring unique strengths, challenges, experiences, and personalities, which serve to bring texture to the fabric of the team.

As we discussed earlier, one process for looking at your team this way is called *employee performance mapping.* Many tools can be used to identify or classify the different archetypes within a team and determine how those archetypes can be used to manage interactions (e.g., Myers-Briggs, DISC, etc.). If you use these tools properly, they can be very effective in helping you manage the dynamics of your team.

Based on the Four Quadrant Leadership model by the Wilfred Jarvis Institute, I developed the Four Quadrants of Leadership (4QL) matrix. The matrix tool uses the two variables I believe can positively effect change within an organization: *leadership* and *performance*. Figure 6.1 shows these variables as a matrix with four quadrants.

- **Leadership Capacity** in this case is defined as the demonstrated capacity to lead or exert significant influence.

- **Performance** is defined as the combination of competence in job skills and high levels of productivity.

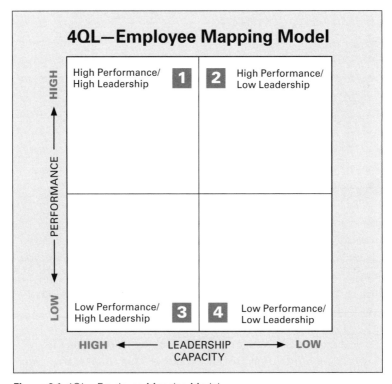

Figure 6.1. 4QL—Employee Mapping Model

Assess your team members on these two factors; then map them into
one of the quadrants. Once all employees are mapped, you can begin
analyzing your organizational texture, identifying both challenges and
strengths.

Looking at Figures 6.2 and 6.3, you see specific cultural trends
emerging through the ratio of employees in the various quadrants;
some trends are positive, and some are not. As the leader, you must be
aware of these trends and be prepared to address them.

- **Creative Synergy.** This state is the ultimate goal for any
  organization. It is a positive, high-energy climate where
  employees and the people they serve are excited and satisfied
  with the progress and results. However, they still seek constant
  improvement and high achievement.

  Your primary role is to encourage and externally champion
  your teams' successes, keep them focused on the vision of the
  district or department, and stay out of their way.

- **Dysfunctional Synergy.** This climate is a leader's worst
  nightmare. It is just the opposite of the previous scenario. It has
  so much organizational inertia that it is extremely difficult to
  effect any real change without a significant turnover in people,
  either through retirement or termination.

  Your primary role here is to outline clearly the department's
  vision and expectations and then make the tough call by determining which personnel need to find satisfaction with another
  organization. Normally, that change will come from employees
  in quadrant 3.

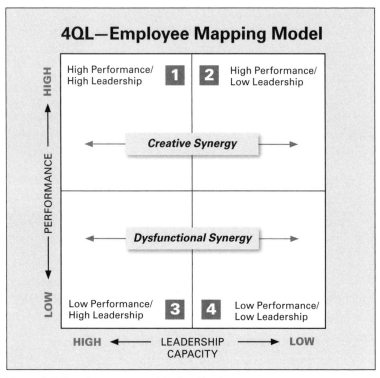

Figure 6.2. Creative synergy and dysfunctional synergy

- **Constant Conflict.** This situation is frustrating but not debilitating for the department *if* you step in and assert appropriate leadership early and often.

You must validate the behaviors of the leaders in quadrant 1 and promote those behaviors as the desired ones for the organization as a whole. Concurrently, you must also recognize the contributions of the people in quadrant 3 from a "skills" perspective in order to avoid further alienating them.

Using good coaching and dialogue techniques, you can help each individual value the others' contributions to the team, a key factor for working together successfully and removing dissonance.

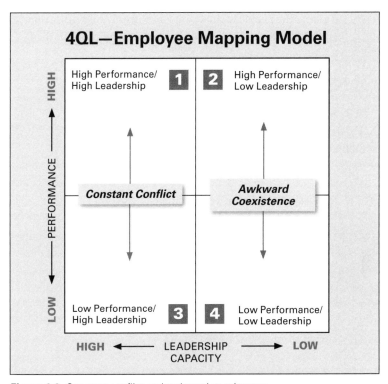

Figure 6.3. Constant conflict and awkward coexistence

- **Awkward Coexistence.** This state is really the easiest to mitigate within your department. The real issue is lack of leadership—period. It is not performance. The low performers probably do not know what high performance means or how to perform well, and they merely need effective leadership to make the transition to high performance.

  You can provide that leadership directly or indirectly to help them identify what the characteristics of high performers are, identify why those characteristics are important, and offer practical strategies to help the employees improve.

Because the people in quadrant 2 are already high performers, you need to increase their leadership capacity to strengthen your team.

Your real goal in this situation is to move the people in quadrant 2 to 1 and those in quadrant 4 to 2.

In Figures 6.4 and 6.5, we see the most interesting culture combinations:

- Constant Frustration and Avoidance/Isolation
- Persistent Frustration and Avoidance/Isolation

These particular sets of interactions are unique in that the two groups are experiencing different outcomes. As a result, the situation often goes unaddressed. Because one group has pulled away, there appears to be no problem or a minimal one. A couple of specific changes will restore a healthy balance to the team.

First, you have to address the frustration.

In Figure 6.4, the people in quadrant 1 are frustrated because they feel those in quadrant 4 are not pulling their weight. You need to help them identify ways to engage the people in quadrant 4 positively. The rising stars have to be willing to model the appropriate behaviors and attitudes for those most at risk. You also need to create opportunities for those quadrant 4 individuals to get a sense of shared purpose and commitment to increase their level of productivity.

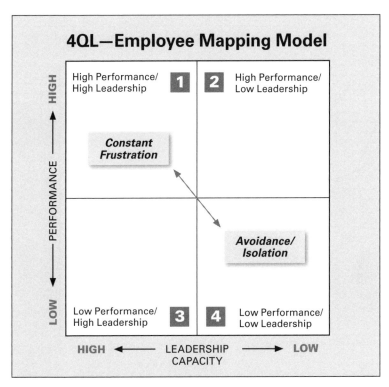

Figure 6.4. Constant frustration and avoidance/isolation

In Figure 6.5, for the people in quadrant 3, the frustration is not what they feel, but what they cause. You must find a way to channel their leadership energies to increase their productivity. When they are left to their own devices, they will use their talents for leadership to create dissonance within your teams. They are not concerned about their performance. As a matter of fact, they will often create contentious situations to hide the fact that they are low performers. In this case, it is best in the short term to let those in quadrant 2 continue to isolate themselves. Otherwise, they could get caught up in dysfunctional behaviors and reduce their productivity.

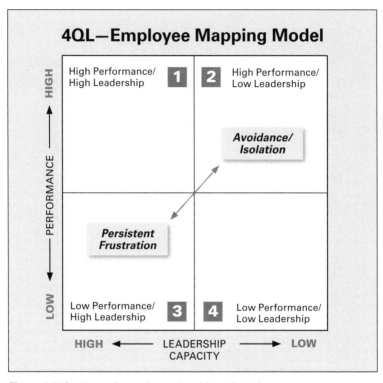

Figure 6.5. Persistent frustration and avoidance/isolation

You must get the groups that pull away and isolate themselves to understand that isolation is not good for the department. Their knowledge and experience are too important to the team as a whole. You must coach them on how to appreciate the differences in the other team members' abilities and approaches as well as how to communicate effectively with their teammates. Allowing avoidance is not an option or long-term solution.

The reason I prefer this type of instrument, instead of a personality assessment tool, is that the variables being assessed can be quantified and modified without telling a person he or she is flawed. This assessment has more to do with professional behaviors and skills, which clearly fall into the domain of responsibility we have as leaders.

Power Questions

- What is the dominant culture in your department or school today? Which quadrants do your people fall into today, and what type of working environment does it create in your department? Is it positive or dissonant?

- Has it always been this way? If not, who do you think has the most impact on changing it?

- What are the last three things you did to move those in quadrant 2 to quadrant 1? How successful were those efforts? Why do you think you had that result?

- What are the last three things you did to move those in quadrant 3 to quadrant 1? How successful were those efforts? Why do you think you had that result?

- What are the last three things you did to move those in quadrant 4 to quadrant 2? How successful were those efforts? Why do you think you had that result?

- For those who made no effort to change quadrants, are you willing to move them out now? If you aren't, why not?

How Is the Boss Doing? Leadership Accountability

We have spent a great deal of time talking about how and why we evaluate and manage the performance of our staff members. Another factor you should carefully consider is your own performance. In other words, how does your staff think you are doing?

In the private sector, these types of evaluations are quite common and are often part of a process called a 360-degree evaluation. In this formal process, the subordinates provide feedback that is incorporated into the evaluation cycle. I am not advocating a 360-degree evaluation here. You can build something much more informal that still serves a valuable purpose for your department or team.

To build an environment that values feedback and uses data as a vital part of an ongoing growth process, you must model for your staff this same desire for and openness to feedback. This step probably sounds quite risky to you. Yet nothing else can provide you with as much valuable insight into how effective you are (versus how effective you think you are).

So, how would you begin to do something like this? Take a look at Activity 9 at the end of this chapter. When I first implemented this process, I gave the survey to my direct reports so they could evaluate me. The second year, we administered this survey to the entire department and had them evaluate the entire IT leadership team, including me. We then collected and analyzed the results. Obviously, your situation will vary based on the size and structure of your department or organization. Another factor you want to consider is the existing level of trust within your group. If it is already high, then you can move through this process much faster.

As you think about implementing this concept, I have one important caution for you. The process must allow for anonymity, especially as you begin. Your staff members must feel complete freedom to give you candid feedback. Yes, it can give them the opportunity to take a few shots at you. If that occurs, then you'll know a fairly serious problem probably exists, and that, too, is valuable feedback.

After getting the results, I would strongly recommend you take plenty of time to review the data privately to understand what it is telling you before you actually meet with any group. You need time to reflect on where your team or staff is coming from before you respond. Allow time for any defensiveness you feel to dissipate.

When you are ready to share the data with others, sit down in small groups, review the data together, and talk about the findings. Focus on trends rather than anomalies or spikes. After all, you cannot change everything at once, so it's best to focus on changes that will affect the most people. Now begin to think about what actions these findings might generate. These discussions are powerful opportunities for change you can bring to your staff. Sometimes the feedback will point to changes the team needs to make, and sometimes it will highlight changes you need to make.

If you authentically and openly work through this process with your team or staff, you will be surprised at how receptive they will be in future conversations regarding their own professional growth and improvement. You have modeled for them how to take constructive feedback appropriately, how to engage in a healthy dialogue about changing behaviors or practices, and how to implement new behaviors or practices as a result of the conferencing process.

How Do You Herd Cats? MBOs and Teams

I grew up in a household where the pets of choice—not mine—were cats and lots of them. I can clearly remember feeding time, as my mother tried to organize them into groups so each group would be eating from the correct bowl of food. It was the proverbial zoo. Sometimes it may seem that way when we try to lead our staff, especially when it comes to focusing their efforts on common outcomes.

As an outgrowth of the Total Quality Management movement, private industry began using management by performance objectives more than 25 years ago. The private sector embraced the concept of performance objectives as a way to increase profitability and accountability. It has dramatically changed the way that employees are evaluated and compensated. It has also changed the nature of what it means to be successful as a leader within the corporate environment.

Today, as education leaders, we are being called upon for greater accountability. For those of us in public education, accountability is often coupled with a dwindling availability of resources. Many public sector organizations have begun to adopt the MBO model. I have used performance objectives in school districts because I believe this method delivers more than increased accountability. This approach provides an authentic way to integrate the strategic planning, operational planning, resource allocation, and professional development aspects of our jobs more uniformly.

However, there is another important aspect to the MBO model. It allows each employee to know how he or she individually contributes to the organization's overall success (or decline). Far too often in large organizations, an employee does not see where his or her particular job fits into the big picture. This can result in a drop in performance unless the employee has a high degree of intrinsic motivation.

Are you ready to implement a performance management program? The first step is to understand that good performance objectives must clearly align with the district's or school's goals. The better the alignment, the better the final results for each employee and the organization.

Using the information presented in the previous chapters, you should now have well-articulated vision and value statements, which is a critical foundation to build upon. You must see them in evidence as you begin the development process for the performance objectives.

The next step is to understand how to craft a meaningful objective. A performance objective is more than a mere laundry list of tasks that an employee expects to accomplish during the course of the year. Instead, it is a set of strategically aligned actions that result in measurable outcomes within a specific time frame. *But* it's not as complicated as it sounds!

Make your objectives SMART:

> **S**pecific
>
> **M**easurable
>
> **A**chievable
>
> **R**esults-oriented
>
> **T**ime-bound

You can use a form similar to Figure 6.6 to help your staff begin working through this process.

Strategic IT Department (District) Goal:		
Performance Objectives	**Indicators of Success**	**Target Completion Date**

Figure 6.6. A tool to track performance objectives

In the form, the key fields are a description of the performance objective, indicators of success, and a target completion date. From experience, I know that unless you have all three elements present, you will not realize the full benefits of this approach.

Focus on Results

When you start using this process, you must consider several key aspects. First, how will you know when you have successfully achieved the objectives? The key here is to measure the *results*—not the *effort*. It is very common for employees and supervisors to spend most of their time trying to evaluate the effort that went into a project. Other times, the evaluation is merely on the end product or service. However, if you are trying to implement a strategic focus for developing your staff and seeking alignment with the district, this narrow focus will likely fall short. Instead, clearly identify the desired results you are seeking by undertaking the particular project or program.

How will this information help you use this template? First, it helps you define the performance objective itself. As you begin writing objectives, make sure they answer "so what?" instead of "what?" For many people, this will require a mental shift.

> A **product** or **service** focus answers the question, "What?" A **results-oriented** focus answers the question, "So what?" or "Why?"

Second, it provides you with a means to measure your performance. Using the template, you are now ready to tackle the indicators-of-success field. Once you have built a solid results-focused objective, you can think about how you will measure whether you achieved those results. Again, this may be very different from the measures of success you and your team are used to. Merely delivering the product or service should not be the only measure of success.

As a CIO, I have found that technical employees especially seem to have a difficult time committing to specific indicators of success. They tend to view the product or service as the success. It is hard for most of them to understand why you would need to consider anything beyond that. Therefore, you will need to give them the support necessary to envision indicators of success beyond products and services.

Getting in Line

Another great aspect of managing by performance objectives is the tight alignment it can bring to your department. This alignment can be seen in the actions of the staff members within the department as well as the department's activities within the district as a whole.

You will notice the first column in Figure 6.6 is where strategic goals are listed. Depending on how you choose to implement the performance objective process, you may begin by aligning with the

IT department's strategic goals or with the district's strategic goals. Which of these you choose will depend on a variety of factors.

If you are part of a school district that has a well-structured strategic planning process, then clearly you will want to align your team's goals with the district's goals. The sooner you can align with the larger organizational goals the better. The home run for your team is when they can clearly see how their work supports the mission and vision of the larger organization and in turn the district can see the value your department provides in helping them achieve the district's strategic goals.

If your district has not been as successful in communicating and institutionalizing its goals, then you might choose instead to focus on aligning with your department goals. Also, if you have not historically spent much time developing a process- or metrics-driven culture in your department, you may want to phase in this new process slowly and limit the focus to your department's goals.

If you are aligning with the larger district goals, then there is something else to consider. In an ideal world, all your performance objectives will align with at least one strategic goal. In reality, there are instances where you have work that is unique to your department and must be done, but that work does not align with the larger organizational goals. That is perfectly OK.

Timing Is Everything

The template facilitates focused accountability by using a *target completion* date field. Two of the points in performance management are that the objectives must be *achievable* and *time-bound*. When you are working with your team and setting target completion dates, the dates should be achievable and realistic. If they are not, you're setting people up for failure. So make sure that when the bar is set, it is not set too high. It's fine to create *stretch* for the employee or the team, but they must be able to reach their goals. Otherwise, you risk demoralizing your staff.

This is another field that tends to give IT staff heartburn. Although some people thrive under timelines and deadlines, others find any type of measure that increases accountability or specificity stressful. You must help everyone understand that only by setting *realistic* timelines for the performance objectives can the department begin to create reasonable action plans, allocate resources, manage customer expectations, and drive increased productivity.

Monitor, Monitor, Monitor

Finally, use the performance objectives as a tool to encourage an ongoing dialogue throughout the year about the direction your department or organization is heading. Are you still on course? It is easy to lose focus, given the number of various crises that can arise in the daily routine. Make sure you're making progress toward your performance objectives in the midst of the tyranny of the urgent.

To paraphrase the old adage, we know how important something really is by how often we check on it. This is certainly true for performance objectives. If you and your team create them at the beginning of the year and then never visit them again until the end-of-year evaluations, you have sent a very clear message about their value. More importantly, the probability of actually achieving any of them will be minimal.

Power Questions

- What drives your department's action plans today?

- How do you measure whether your action plan is successful now? Is it measured on delivery of a product or service? Quality of effort? Result? How do you know?

- How do your department goals and objectives align with those of the superintendent or other senior administrators?

Grow or Perish: PGPs and Teams

One of the first rules I learned in biology was that any living organism that is not growing is dying or dead. That same rule can apply to us as professionals as well. Given the rate of change within today's society, we have to keep learning and growing in order to meet the increased demands of the evolving workplace. As a leader, you have the responsibility of ensuring your staff learns and grows, too.

One of the new strategies becoming commonplace in the workforce is the professional growth plan (PGP). PGPs are not the same as professional improvement plans (PIPs), which are typically associated with low-performing employees. They do not serve the same purpose or share the same attributes.

PGPs yield three primary benefits:

1. Provide direct benefits to employees in terms of extending their professional value and achieving personal and professional goals, which can include enhancing their career advancement opportunities.

2. Provide significant value to your organization in terms of increased productivity, performance, and quality of work from employees.

3. Provide a mechanism by which you can foster a professional learning community within your team or department.

For many CIOs, the idea of professional growth begins and ends with the evaluation cycle. True, this process is an important component of a good professional growth program. It brings the elements of accountability, reflection, and goal setting into the discussion in a structured manner. However, evaluations alone are not sufficient.

Professional growth plans are a strategy for engaging employees at a whole new level and bringing them to a better understanding of who they are, where they want to go, and what they can and should bring to the organization. When PGPs are coupled with an effective evaluation process, you have a powerful program for motivating staff to levels of performance that will probably astound you.

How to Build a PGP 101

Select a tool that will help you work through this process with your staff. The tool should be designed to make it easy to facilitate this practice. Remember the old rule of thumb: "form follows function."

A typical PGP contains several key fields, including the following:

- Career goals—including both short- and long-term time frames

- Employees' strengths/areas for growth—including both self-assessed and supervisor-assessed

- Areas of interest—job-related knowledge domains and areas of high interest identified by the employee

- Preferred learning styles—to be ranked by the employee

- Opportunities for leadership—action plans related to strengths

- Opportunities for growth—action plans related to areas needing improvement

- Opportunities for enrichment—action plans related to areas of high interest

- Stretch opportunity (optional)—action plans to accomplish a goal that benefits the department or organization but that is not within the scope of the employee's job

To implement this strategy, you must understand what you are capable of providing to your employees. By this I mean, what are you already capable of doing to help them grow professionally, and how will you need to supplement your skill set with outside resources?

This issue gets back to the heart of the leadership models in chapter 2. Although you know you have the responsibility to grow your staff, you may realize that this is not within your core competencies or that you have specific skill gaps yourself. You cannot let your staff's needs go unfulfilled because of your own shortcomings.

You need to have a good understanding of what types of resources are available to assist you. These resources may come from other departments within your organization, or they may be totally external. Do not be afraid to reach out to other departments within your district. This is a great way to strengthen relationships.

As you build your potential resource bank, think of the various ways you could use these resources to support professional growth for your staff. Also think about how you could offer your team's expertise in return to supplement other departments' professional growth programs. This give-and-take approach is the best way to build strong bridges that can assist you in other areas of your technology program execution.

Power Questions

- Besides sending your staff to training courses, how do you manage their professional growth? How is their personal growth tied to their evaluation?

- How would a formal PGP change the nature of your department if implemented as outlined?

- Who in your organization could assist you in setting up a process like a PGP?

The Sensei's Parting Thoughts

- Leaders must develop leadership capacity in the team and be accountable for the performance of the team.

- Leaders must align expectations for staff performance with the department's, school's, or district's vision.

- Leaders must accept the responsibility to help everyone succeed.

- Management by Objectives (MBO) programs are effective ways to focus a team and align its work with that of the greater organization.

- Well-structured performance objectives must be SMART: specific, measurable, achievable, results-oriented, and time-bound.

- Professional Growth Plans (PGPs) are one strategy for moving beyond the traditional annual evaluation process to better develop leadership and overall competence in your staff.

Managing the performance of your department or school involves much more than merely conducting annual personnel evaluations. It is really about managing expectations, standards, direction, and relationships. Effectively managing the performance of your team will require:

- a clear vision of where you want them to go,

- a clear understanding that you cannot do it alone,

- a personal commitment to success for all members of your team,

- a clear understanding that accountability is necessary and fair, and

- a clear acceptance that diversity within your team is both its greatest challenge and its greatest strength.

practical activities

Activity 9　■　**Management Quality Survey**

This survey is designed to help you to assess the leadership climate within your department or team. It can be used to assess you personally, a team's immediate supervisor, the department's total leadership team, or even the district's leadership team. I would caution that the further removed you are from the day-to-day activities of those being surveyed, the less valid the feedback will be.

Another important factor to consider is to *ensure the confidentiality* of each person responding to the survey. You must not ask for feedback in a way that allows for individually identifiable responses. You want honest, candid feedback so you and your team can identify areas for improvement. The goal is not to feel good or bad; it is to find areas to target for improvement.

Once you have finished the survey, it is vital that you analyze the data. Identify the trends, both positive and negative. Then report back to the group that took the time and risk to give you the feedback. Let them know what areas will be targeted for follow-up action. Finally, let them know when you plan to conduct another survey to see whether things are improving. You want them to know you listened, are doing something about any problems, and will check back with them to see if the proposed solutions are working. This is how you gain a high level of trust and respect.

If you are not willing to do all three of these things, do not bother doing this activity at all. Your time is too valuable, and you can better use it elsewhere.

The following are helpful guidelines for making this activity successful:

- The process must have a predictable frequency so that you can take advantage of trend analysis. You will get some negative feedback—expect it, work on it, and watch it get better.

- The process should include a report presented back to the team that provided the input. That way they know you did something with their feedback; otherwise, they will not take the process seriously the next time.

- Before you read through the responses, have handy your favorite dessert or means of comfort. You can guarantee that a few people will take this opportunity to vent or take pot shots. After reading the comments, enjoy your dessert and give yourself time to process the information.

- Celebrate the areas of success.

- After reading the surveys, do something you enjoy, and don't dwell on the negative.

- Finally, create a time-bound, measurable action plan for how to improve deficient areas.

Instructions

1. Distribute the Management Quality Survey to the targeted group. Giving it to them in an electronic format to fill in on the computer, then print off and hand in, allows for an extra level of anonymity.

2. Provide a deadline for completion and a point person to whom they are to return the completed surveys. It should not be you or your administrative assistant.

3. After the deadline, collect the surveys from the point person or collection area, and begin the data analysis. Compile the findings and chart the results. Look for trends.

4. Summarize the top three strengths and the top three areas for improvement. Share them with your survey participants.

5. Identify and announce a follow-up survey date.

ACTIVITY 9 ▪ WORKSHEET 1

Management Quality Survey

In our ongoing efforts to improve the quality of management, we are asking you to complete this survey. Please rate the IT Leadership Team's overall performance in each of the areas listed.

For each survey item in the following table, circle the number to the right that best fits your judgment of its quality. Use the scale below to select the quality number. Also indicate the trend for each area: (↑) means things are going *better*, (↓) means things are *slipping*, no arrow circled means *status quo*.

1	Needs significant improvement
2	Still needs improvement
3	Overall OK
4	Well done
5	Definitely an area of strength

Description / Identification of Survey Item	Scale					Trend
Teamwork	1	2	3	4	5	⬇ ⬆
Internal communication	1	2	3	4	5	⬇ ⬆
Employee involvement	1	2	3	4	5	⬇ ⬆
Employee recognition	1	2	3	4	5	⬇ ⬆
Cross-departmental collaboration	1	2	3	4	5	⬇ ⬆
Delegation of authority and tasks	1	2	3	4	5	⬇ ⬆
Clarity of goals	1	2	3	4	5	⬇ ⬆
Encourages change and growth	1	2	3	4	5	⬇ ⬆
Attention to quality	1	2	3	4	5	⬇ ⬆
Accomplishment of goals	1	2	3	4	5	⬇ ⬆
Work relationship with customers/users	1	2	3	4	5	⬇ ⬆
External communication	1	2	3	4	5	⬇ ⬆
Staff skill building	1	2	3	4	5	⬇ ⬆
Consistency of words and actions	1	2	3	4	5	⬇ ⬆
Openness to new ideas and feedback	1	2	3	4	5	⬇ ⬆

Activity 10 ▪ How Everyday Leaders Create Extraordinary Workplaces

We spent a great deal of time in this chapter talking about performance and evaluation. We looked at a number of ways to measure performance. We also examined the various roles you as the leader take on in helping to manage your staff through the growth, performance, and evaluation processes. There are still other things you can do as the leader that directly impact the performance levels of your staff members and shape the climate of the workplace.

This activity is designed to gather input from your leadership staff (team leaders) so you can identify the most powerful ways you can assist them by creating a positive workplace that empowers them to succeed. The goal is to get those who serve in leadership roles within your department, whether formally (such as directors, coordinators, managers, etc.) or in more informal roles (team leaders, project leaders, building-level instructional technology coordinators, etc.) to look at what is happening in your department now with a critical and reflective eye.

This tool serves as a framework that can launch quality dialogue for changing policies and processes within your department. These changes can have a lasting impact long after the activity itself is concluded. But don't make this a one-time event. The real benefit lies in making this an ongoing practice. No matter how good you are now, there is always room for improvement.

ACTIVITY 10 ■ WORKSHEET 1

How Everyday Leaders Create Extraordinary Workplaces

Your team's success—in good times or bad—ultimately depends on the knowledge, skills, and commitment of your employees. Connect with them, and they will develop solutions and relationships that allow you to thrive in any situation.

Reflect on each statement, and with your team identify two specific action steps you will take within the next 30 days and record them below.

1. **Show the connection.** Ensure that every employee is able to see how his or her job contributes to the success of team members and the entire operation. Interdependent partnerships create a feeling of ownership that enhances relationships and increases results.

   1. _____

   2. _____

2. **Remove a barrier every 30 to 60 days.** Ask your staff to identify and prioritize the obstacles that prevent their good performance. Commit to removing one barrier every 30 to 60 days until the list has been exhausted. Begin with those that can be accomplished quickly and provide visible results.

   1. _____

   2. _____

3. **Make recognition and encouragement a priority.** Frequent, honest, and specific recognition should be the norm. There is no need to wait for performance that exceeds expectations.

   1. _____

   2. _____

4. **Ensure system alignment.** Policies and practices inconsistent with organizational value statements are a leading cause of distrust. Evaluate key processes and systems to determine those that keep you from connecting with employees. Performance management, selection, and incentive systems are a good place to begin.

   1. _____

   2. _____

5. **Don't forget the majority.** Your team can be classified into three basic groups. The stars are at one end of the continuum. Those who need to make substantial improvement or else move on are at the other. The majority lie somewhere in the middle. They provide the foundation for your team's success. Dramatic results can occur with small, incremental improvements within this middle group.

   1. _____

   2. _____

Activity 11 ■ **Quadrant Mapping Staff Performance**

The reasoning behind mapping employees into quadrants is twofold:

1. You can easily identify clusters of employees that have common needs for professional growth activities and/or have strengths to offer teammates as mentors or coaches.

2. You can identify potential reasons for performance issues within teams or between particular individuals in the department to develop appropriate intervention strategies.

Quadrant mapping also allows you to identify where you need to invest more of your time in directly mentoring or coaching your rising stars. They are critical to your ongoing success.

Review the 4QL—Employee Mapping Model (see Figure 6.1 on page 144) and description of the employee mapping model process. Also review the quandrant patterns, which are shown in Figures 6.2 through 6.5 on pages 146–150.

Assess each of your employees on performance and leadership capacity then map them into appropriate quadrants on the chart. The reasoning behind this mapping is twofold:

1. You can easily identify clusters of employees who have common needs for professional growth activities and/or have strengths to offer teammates as mentors or coaches.

2. You can identify potential reasons for performance issues within teams or between particular individuals in the department to develop appropriate intervention strategies.

The 4QL—Employee Mapping Model also allows you to identify where you need to invest more of your time in directly mentoring or coaching your rising stars. They are critical to your ongoing success. When is the best time to conduct this performance assessment and mapping? You might find the following times most valuable.

- One of the most practical times to conduct this activity is just before the various evaluation cycles. It gives you a way to track progress over time with the individuals that remain within your department for extended periods. By pulling out the charts you used in the past, you can easily see their histories. This can lead you to ask several important questions:

  Are they on a positive path? What behaviors support that perception? Does that match the evaluation you are about to conduct? Finally, what can be done either to continue the positive changes or to reverse a decline?

- You can use this same tool before you assign personnel to a project, especially if the project team will be large. It will help you think about the dynamics of the team and the ways they will probably interact, long before they begin their work. It gives you the opportunity to be proactive in developing strategies to assist the team and avoid potential problems before they occur.

- This tool can also be helpful during the course of the project when problems arise. You can map out the team members or stakeholders involved and try to understand the dynamics. This process can often give you a clue about where to start the intervention. Most problems are really more about relationships than about technical or content knowledge.

- Finally, often you will experience staff changes during the summer, because this is a natural transition period for families with the beginning and ending of school. With personnel turnover, the composition of your team may change, and so may your team dynamic. When you are ready to begin a new school year, you can use this tool to assess your staff mix and climate. It can help you understand what you need to do with a new team to provide the best leadership and a positive climate.

chapter 7

can you
hear me now?

*Many attempts
to communicate
are nullified
by saying too much.*

Robert Greenleaf,
Director of Management Research, AT&T

Max's Journey

Max walked into class with a spring in his step. His team had had a successful week, and he believed his new leadership knowledge was really starting to pay off. The wireless project was finally showing excellent progress, and the anxiety from staff in the schools had dropped noticeably. Also, the server migration project was nearly complete, and the team seemed to be working together better—even Stan, who at first had been struggling to find his place. Max felt hopeful for the first time in quite a while.

As he took his seat, he was pleased to see Professor Oracle. He had done a complete about-face on her during the course of the semester. Although her particular style of leadership was very distinct from his, he had learned to appreciate the skill set she brought to the table. She obviously was quite gifted in her own right, and he had to admit that he had learned a lot from her.

Professor Oracle greeted the class with her typically cheery demeanor as she took her place in the circle.

"Clearly, if I were to ask any of you about the importance of effective communication in leadership, you would list it near the top of your priorities. Inevitably, when stakeholders are polled about areas where they want their leaders to improve, it shows up near the top of their concerns, too. Today we will explore practical ways you can tackle this issue in your department or organization.

"Some of the specific aspects of communications we will tackle are understanding the importance and benefits of effective communication, understanding the characteristics that define effective communication, and identifying strategies that can enhance your communications programs."

Max took out his laptop and began taking notes.

Theory

So what exactly is effective communication? If that is our goal, and I believe we all agree this is something we must strive to achieve, then we need to begin by understanding what effective communication is and what it is not.

Defining Communication

At its most basic level, communication is the exchange of information from one party to another party in such a manner that it is relevant and understandable. As we explore this topic, this definition will be used as the context for our discussion.

In this basic definition, there are four key factors that must always be present in order for real communication to occur.

1. Information must be present.

2. There must be more than one party in the exchange.

3. The medium used for the exchange of information must be appropriate.

4. The final message must be relevant and understandable to the receiving party.

Points one through three may seem fairly obvious. But it is point number four that often determines whether the communication is truly effective or not. Point number three strongly affects point number four, because there are so many different media possible for the delivery of the message.

The next aspect to understand in communications is how to shape the message itself by considering the basic components of communication: audience, purpose, message, intended action, and key take-away. Careful reflection on these components during the planning phase is fundamental to successful communications. The following list provides some guiding questions to assist you in crafting an appropriate communications message or plan.

Audience. Who is the primary group(s) you are going to address, and what is the most appropriate medium(s) to reach them?

Purpose. What is the primary purpose for this contact at this particular time? Is your purpose clearly defined in your mind?

Message. What is the key message(s) you want them to know, and why is it important to them? Is it relevant and understandable for your primary audience? Why would they want to take their time to pay attention to it?

Intended Action. What action do you want them to take after this communication (if any)? What action do you not want them to take (if any)?

Key Take-Away. What is the last thing you want them to remember and possibly share with their neighbor? What is the sound bite?

One of the greatest dangers technologists face in the area of communications is the lure of the technology. Because we generally are not afraid of it, we like to explore the new and innovative. As a result, we incorporate many flashy techniques into our nonprint communication strategies, hoping to increase the impact of the message. Unfortunately, the opposite usually occurs.

The recipients of the message may very well be entertained or impressed with the visual cleverness or effect and wonder how you did it. However, more often than not, they will not walk away with your key message. It gets lost in the glitz. When this happens, you did not communicate.

Now that you understand the fundamental principles behind effective communication, lets move on to the practical application and dig deeper.

Power Questions

- From which medium(s) do you prefer to receive your information—print, video, TV, radio, Internet?

- In which medium(s) are you most skilled at communicating? How do you share these skills with your peers?

- In which medium(s) do you need the most development? How are you acquiring these competencies?

Application

Schools and districts are grappling with diminishing resources while trying to respond to increased demands for public accountability. This increased public scrutiny causes educational executives to be more sensitive to all expenditures. They must be able to explain why any spending was a good use of public money. When resources are spent for technology, especially in areas that are not directly related to classroom technology, it can be very difficult for superintendents and other executives to articulate the value of technology to their boards and other constituents.

As technology leaders, we are tasked with managing one of the more complex and costly areas of school operations. Unfortunately, it only continues to increase in both of those aspects. That very fact often makes us the target of sometimes undeserved negative criticism, skepticism, and blanket attacks about the value we provide to our districts. So when budget preparation time rolls around, many of us find ourselves in uncomfortably defensive positions. We regularly have to explain why a particular service or staffing allocation is critical in keeping the department afloat.

I would suggest that criticism and skepticism from others does not actually stem from them thinking that the technology department is unimportant. It's more likely that they simply do not understand what it does. Consider: Have you provided significant ongoing communication about the value your department or team provides to the community? Was your communication effective?

If you don't have an effective ongoing communications program in place, then as the technology leader you may face demands to reduce your budget. The resources you hoped to get for IT will be rerouted to areas that are more easily understood by the executive team and the public. Budgeting for IT is really not an issue of actual value, but whether the value is being effectively articulated and communicated to decision makers.

Create multiple ways to collect your team's successes and keep them highly visible to internal and external stakeholders.

- *Success wall*
- *Department blog*
- *Project website*
- *Video presentation in a kiosk*
- *Electronic newsletter*

We also must use communication to celebrate our successes. Organizations have an emotional culture, and that culture must be carefully managed. When the emotional culture is positive, the organization often can move forward more quickly in achieving its goals. One key component in maintaining this positive emotional state is to celebrate successes. Unfortunately, as IT leaders we often are too busy fighting fires or moving on to the next project to step back and enjoy a moment of success. This is a major mistake. It is the energy derived from this celebration that helps propel the organization to its next milestone with a high degree of positive anticipation. An effective communications program involves your department or district in the celebration of successes.

So, as you can see, there are several practical reasons to develop and maintain an ongoing communications program within your technology program. As the leader, you must not only set the expectation for this to occur, you must also take the lead to see that it actually happens. Now, the next challenge is determining what to say.

Find Your Story

If you review the work plans for most IT departments for a year, you think, "How in the world are they going to get all that done in one year?" That can be the problem when it comes to telling your story, too. Sometimes we want to tell our audience *everything* we are doing, and ultimately, we end up telling them *nothing*. The most important thing you can do when building your communications plan is to figure out "What is core?"

Ask yourself these questions:

- What is it that you are going to focus on?
- What do you ultimately want to be known for doing really well?
- What are you passionate about?

That is where you begin finding your story. As a CIO, I took a department through this process. We chose to focus on technology's role in helping us achieve three things:

1. Equity in learning opportunity
2. Students as leaders and learners
3. Instructional significance as core

It is also important to determine what you are *not* going to continue talking about. As technology people, we love to talk about how many computers we have installed, routers we have replaced, or miles of fiber optic network cable are in place. The question that always comes to mind when I start reading material like this is, "So what?"

How is this going to make a difference to my kid, say in helping her get into college or find a good job? As a technology leader, you can't assume your audience cares about what you care about. Remember you are communicating for *them*, not yourself.

Sell Your Story

Sometimes I think it surprises technology leaders that a big part of our jobs is to be a sort of salesperson, selling decision makers on our projects and the services we provide. One of the best ways to do that is through an effective communications program. The following are several key factors in making your communications campaign more effective.

Delivery

- Identify your key audiences—both internal and external.

- Use multiple mediums as you deliver the messages.

- Communicate on a consistent and predictable basis.

- Communicate at the level and in the manner they will understand (put your pride and educational and technical lingo away).

Design/Branding

- Find powerful visual images to reinforce your key messages— pictures are noticed more than words.

- Students are powerful components in delivering your message when they can honestly say they've benefited.

- Develop a catch phrase that captures minds and hearts, and then use it in all communication to help instantly identify your department.

Content

- Focus more on why a particular project is helping instruction and students and less on the technology.

- Skew the balance to *stories* (the human side of how you are making a difference) rather than *news*.

- Keep your stakeholders aware of where you are going next; you want them to own the vision and be excited about it.

So, how can you use these guidelines?

- Build a communications plan with an understanding that your audiences are composed of all stakeholders within your school district. This includes those people who reside in your community with and without children in your schools.

- Construct a layered approach to sharing information that uses print, video, Internet, surveys, community forums, open-houses, and other special events.

- Sponsor activities to showcase your students and the instructional changes and progress occurring within your district.

- Partner with the Instructional Services and the Public Relations departments on activities, and begin viewing them as valued allies.

- Chose a theme that has a powerful meaning within your community to become your communications brand, and use it consistently.

How do I know this will work? Because this outline was the framework of the initial plan in my district, and our community continues to support our technology program actively to this day. It can work for you, too. Don't feel like you have to implement every idea all at once. But you've got to start somewhere.

Defining the Message

I'm sure you're asking yourself, "What is the payoff for doing all this work?" If you put forth the effort to create a quality communications program, the rewards can be significant.

First, your stakeholders, both internal and external, become much more engaged in your work and own the vision you are striving to bring to reality. The importance of this cannot be overestimated. It is not enough that you have a clear picture of where you want to take your department or district. Everyone else affected needs to understand the vision and also want to go there. It makes removing barriers you encounter along the way and finding advocates to support you so much easier.

That brings us to the second benefit. Now that districts and schools are faced with continually dwindling resources, a shared vision yields a stronger support base to generate continued funding. It takes you out of the position of constantly having to resell your vision and every single project on its individual merits.

When you genuinely communicate with your stakeholders, your staff and students will feel supported and valued. They will know their efforts are recognized and appreciated. The ability to celebrate success is vitally important to maintaining a positive climate within your organization, and your communications efforts can be a tremendous asset in achieving that goal. Again, this may not seem like a traditional role for an IT leader, but it is one that a shrewd technology professional will not ignore.

All of these benefits combine to create one last systemic benefit—your organization will make significant leaps in achieving its vision. This statement may sound like hyperbole; however, certain fundamental components cannot be ignored when trying to achieve something as lofty as a vision. You must have shared agreement for the direction, an appropriate level of resources, organizational momentum, and staff and leadership commitment. When all these factors align, you can take mammoth strides forward in reaching those aggressive goals you developed. Your communications plan is essential to laying a solid foundation for making that possible.

The Rest of the Story

Now you understand the need, have some strategies to find your story, know how to sell it, and understand what happens when you do. I am sure you are wondering how you begin the planning process for building a communications plan. I suggest starting by answering the following brainstorming questions:

- What did we really accomplish that was important for teaching and learning?

- How are students highlighted in a positive way?

- Why would I care about this project or activity if I didn't work for the department?

- What medium should we use to communicate our message?

- Why is this medium the best one to use to communicate this message?

This approach to communications is actually fairly simple. Effective communication is about knowing what you want to say and to whom. It is also about forming the habit of doing it on such a regular basis that people expect your communications and enjoy hearing from you.

You will know you have succeeded the first time you miss a communication, and some of your stakeholders comment to you that they really missed your update. The grand slam comes when you are in a budget hearing and a community member or two stands up and quotes back your own information as a rationale for why your funding should be sustained or increased.

Power Questions

- What is your department's story? What would you like it to be?

- How effectively have you branded your department? What does the brand say about your team? How do your actions align with the message?

- How effective have your communication strategies been this year? What measures have you used to determine this?

The Sensei's Parting Thoughts

- It is not effective communication unless the message is relevant, understandable, and sent through a medium appropriate for the receiver.

- The lack of support you experience within your organization is often a result of a poor communications program rather than a reflection of your perceived value as a department.

- Find your story, sell your story, and celebrate your story.

practical activities

Activity 12 ▪ **Communications Audit**

In order to improve your communications strategies, first you need to get a clear understanding of where you are now. That first step is a communications audit.

This exercise is designed to take an objective look at your communications activities over the past year. This process, often called *artifact analysis*, is effective in helping identify consistent and common errors.

An audit also identifies where to focus your improvement efforts to yield the greatest immediate benefits. It is one thing to understand the concepts of good communication and another to see it exemplified in your own work.

The following are helpful hints:

- Be sure to include samples targeted for your internal stakeholders (district staff) and external stakeholders (community members, vendors, the press, etc.)

- Get communication samples from multiple forms of media. (print, screen shots of Web-based communications, even short video clips if practical)

- The recommended structure for this activity is a collection of small groups. The synergy that occurs in having multiple points of view conducting the analysis is quite powerful. If you do this exercise in a small group setting, make sure each member of the group has a sheet for each communication sample you intend to review.

- You can conduct this audit on your own if you desire; it will still be valuable.

Instructions

1. Have the groups select a sampling of the most important communication efforts from the past year. Four to seven samples are recommended.

2. Distribute Activity 12—Worksheet 1 to each participant to use as the groups evaluate the selected communications samples. It is designed to help them evaluate their work for specific criteria that will be used for all samples.

3. Ask the groups to assess the communication samples for each of the key factors listed on the evaluation form.

4. After completing analysis of the samples, have the small groups or the large group discuss the findings.

Key questions to consider include the following:

- What are the key trends found in the evidence?

- Are there obvious gaps in your communications program— are there stakeholders who are not addressed at all, or inappropriately, too often, and so on?

- Where are you doing a good job now? Why do you think that is the case?

- Based on the data you see, what are the implications if no changes are made in your communications approach?

- Where should your team begin to focus your initial improvement efforts?

Build a communications action plan that identifies practical steps you and your team can implement in the next thirty days, ninety days, and six months.

ACTIVITY 12   ■   WORKSHEET 1

Communications Audit

Sample number	1	2	3
Format Print (P) Online (O) Video (V)			
Description of sample			
Intended audience Internal (I) External (E)			
Primary intended purpose			
Good design elements observed Yes (Y) No (N)			
Message had strong connection to instruction and/or students Yes (Y) No (N)			
Message focused on results or effect on people instead of news about products, services, or projects Yes (Y) No (N)			
Perception of effectiveness for the communication Very—Blue Effective—Green Moderately—Yellow Not—Red			
Evaluation measure used? Yes (Y) No (N)			

Activity 13 ▪ **Finding Your Story**

One of the most difficult tasks in building an effective communications plan is deciding on a clear, focused message. This can be especially challenging for technology leaders educating their stakeholder community about the value of IT. Although we inherently know the value of educational technology, it can be problematic finding the right words to clearly convey the value to all our audiences.

One way to accomplish this complex process is to conduct a group exercise where you delve into important questions: What is driving your department? What would you like to be recognized for doing well? Why should your users care about what you do? These questions may seem quite basic, but you need to be able to answer them in a compelling fashion and in terms that a layperson can understand.

EXERCISE ONE: FINDING THE KEY MESSAGES

Activity 13—Worksheet 1 and Worksheet 2 are designed to provide a framework for leading a brainstorming session about these questions with your team or department. The questions are provided as starting points. You may add others that provide the needed focus for your group.

The following are helpful tips for maximizing learning from both activities:

- Distribute this form to your group a couple of days prior to actually conducting the session. This provides enough time for them to think about the questions. The ability to reflect on these questions before jumping into the discussion is vital.

- Let your team wrestle with the questions and issues—don't jump in and provide answers and guidance too soon. Working through disagreements leads to quality dialogue.

- Allow the group to add new questions for discussion. Adding questions demonstrates that they are internalizing the process and working to provide a meaningful context.

- Accept that you may not come to full closure at the conclusion of this exercise. As the leader, you must assume responsibility for ensuring that follow up conversations occur at some point in the future.

EXERCISE TWO: FRAMING A COMMUNICATIONS PLAN

The goal of this exercise is to help your team think about stakeholders and communications media used by your department. Each group should use Activity 13—Worksheet 2 to direct the brainstorming session.

The final outcome of the exercise provides the building blocks needed for producing a formal communications plan. This activity also develops a call to action. If you want this activity to be a worthwhile investment, you need to walk away with a plan that can produce positive results. Please also review the bullet points in the description of Exercise One.

ACTIVITY 13 ■ WORKSHEET 1

Finding Your Story
EXERCISE ONE: FINDING THE KEY MESSAGES

Use the following questions to direct your brainstorming session:

1. What are our team's achievements with regard to educational technology that we think are *really* worth talking about?

2. What are the *key messages* that we would like to communicate about these achievements?

3. What *difference* have they made in the practice of teaching and learning and in the lives of our students?

Take a look at your answers. Now, imagine effectively sharing these key ideas with a diverse audience in a large-group setting.

4. Does thinking about a different audience change what you would have identified?

5. With this new audience in mind, what are the key messages, and how would you go about communicating them?

ACTIVITY 13 ■ WORKSHEET 2

Finding Your Story

EXERCISE TWO: FRAMING A COMMUNICATIONS PLAN

Part A

Use the following questions to direct your brainstorming session:

1. Who are the stakeholder groups with whom we want to build ongoing communications links?

2. What are the specific outcomes we are seeking in communicating with each group?

3. What are the best delivery media for each group?

4. What were the most effective strategies used in the past? Why?

5. What were the least effective strategies used in the past? Why?

Identify three specific outcomes we will focus on within our communications program this year. What indicators will we use to measure their success?

Part B

In your small group, brainstorm about specific activities that can help us reach the three outcomes you identified.

List at least three specific measurable communication strategies per group. Record each strategy separately on an index card.

Select a reporter to conduct a report out to the large group. Post the strategy cards on the wall.

After all the strategies have been posted on the wall, each person will vote for four specific strategies by posting a dot on the cards of his or her choice. The items with the most votes will form the core of the departmental communications plan for this year.

chapter 8

---

what does it take
to be a great leader?

*The real questions
are the ones that obtrude
upon your consciousness
whether you like it or not,
the ones that make your mind
start vibrating like a jackhammer,
the ones that you 'come to
terms with' only to discover
that they are still there.*

Ingrid Bengis, author

Max's Journey

As Max sat in his office reading weekly status reports, he couldn't help but feel a sense of pride. The project teams had made significant progress. In his ongoing interactions with them, Max saw the dynamics within the teams had definitely shifted to be more positive and productive. They were now clearly operating in the performing stage. It was amazing to see how things had changed over the past five months.

Yes, there were still days he wanted to bang his head against the nearest wall, but those were few and far between. He enjoyed coming to work and felt like most of his staff shared this excitement as well.

He heard a soft knock at the door and looked up to see Stan in the doorway, smiling. Max returned the smile, saying, "Hey, Stan, what can I do for you?"

"I just wanted to let you know that our team just met with the directors' group. We think we have a solution for what they want to accomplish. I'll have a proposal for them to review by the end of the day tomorrow. If you have the time to look it over in the morning, that'd be helpful."

"I'd be happy to. Thanks for jumping on this and helping them out. I know you and the team did a great job. I look forward to seeing your solution." Stan walked away, head held high, smiling.

Max thought to himself, *I'm really glad he's a part of our team.*

Looking down at his watch, Max pushed his chair away from his desk and quickly grabbed his coat. Dashing out of the office and jumping into his car, he headed to the university to meet with Professor Sensei.

Max headed into the familiar gray stone building and briskly walked down the silent hallways. The students were still gone for winter break, and his footsteps echoed in the empty corridors. To him, these halls now felt like a second home.

When he knocked on the professor's door, a familiar voice beckoned him to come in. Professor Sensei sat down in his favorite chair. "Max, it's good to see you. Have you enjoyed your break?" he inquired, motioning for Max to have a seat.

Settling into one of the large, overstuffed chairs, Max laughed briefly. "Well, you know better than that. In a school district technology department, there is no such thing as a real break. When teachers and students are gone, those are optimum times for us to get large-scale projects accomplished. So, I would say it was a productive break."

The professor took on a more serious tone. "You've finished the first stage in your journey, and you've been an excellent student. Now it's my turn to ask you, what does it take to be a good leader?"

Max pondered for a moment, searching for the right words. The last thing he wanted to do was disappoint his mentor. Finally, after a lengthy silence, he said, "A good leader must establish a clear, compelling vision for where he or she is going to take the organization and why they are going there. Then he or she must encourage all stakeholders to see their roles in helping the goals become reality.

"A good leader knows that the people under his or her charge are valuable resources who must be developed and managed to provide long-term organization success. When the leader cares about his team's individual and collective professional growth and success, then the compelling vision the leader has set forth can be achieved.

"A leader is a person who has the ability to ask the right questions, especially the hard ones, and a person who is willing to listen objectively to the answers, even the ones he or she doesn't want to hear. Then the leader needs to ensure that appropriate follow up occurs by wisely leveraging all the resource at his or her disposal.

"Finally, a leader is the person who owns the responsibility for all of the team's outcomes—good and bad."

Professor Sensei listened intently as Max spoke. Then there was another moment of silence. Finally the professor smiled, responding, "You've come full circle. The answers you sought didn't lie in others, but in yourself. Our role was to help you discover them. That is also your role as the leader of your team.

"So where do you go from here?"

Max thought for a moment. "Well, I noticed that Professor Oracle and Professor Sage are teaching a couple of classes next term. So I thought I'd see what new questions I might learn."

Professor Sensei smiled.

Power Questions

- What would this type of leadership change look like in your organization?
- What would it take for it to occur in your organization?
- What changes will it require in you personally?
- What are the three things that you will do now that will have the highest impact?

Conclusion

We, too, have come full circle. What are you going to do next? We have explored a wide variety of topics in this book, and I have tried to provide you with tools to expand the strategies at your disposal.

We learned there are three basic leadership archetypes (sage, sensei, and oracle). They all have specific behavior characteristics, and many people are a blend of more than one type. Each leadership type has positive aspects. We must monitor the negative aspects of the sage and oracle, or we risk creating organizations that do not thrive.

We examined the leader's role in these processes:

- visioning,
- aligning to the core mission,
- team building,
- evaluation and performance management, and
- communication.

We examined new conceptual models for thinking and decision making, including:

- leadership continuum model (LCM),
- reflective leader pyramid,
- student artifact analysis method (SAAM) of assessment model,
- development cycle of teams, and
- 4-quadrant leadership (4QL) model for staff performance.

Now it's your turn for action.

- Go back and review any notes you made to see if any ideas struck you as valuable.

- Make a list of the top three to five activities that you think you would like to try with your team or department. Give yourself a deadline for each activity.

- Select one colleague with whom to share a couple of ideas from the book that resonated during your reading. By discussing ideas with peers, you internalize the ideas and are more likely actually to do something with them.

- Schedule a reminder in your e-mail or task management program for three months and six months from now to check up on whether you implemented the things you wanted to try. It is an easy accountability measure.

Thank you for taking the time to explore these topics. I am honored that you chose to invest your valuable time in this manner. I wish you the very best as you work to improve the educational experience for the students in our country. You are a leader, and you have already taken the first step. Best wishes as you continue your journey.

Bibliography

Collins, J. (2001). *Good to great: Why some companies make the leap . . . And others don't.* New York: HarperCollins Publishers, Inc.

Covey, S. R. (1989). *The seven habits of highly effective people: Restoring the character ethic.* New York: Simon & Schuster Inc.

Feigenbaum, A. V. (1951). *Quality control: Principles, practice, and administration.* New York: McGraw-Hill.

Fisher, R., & Ury, W. (1981). *Getting to yes: Negotiating agreement without giving in.* Boston: Houghton Mifflin.

Gray, J. (1992). *Men are from mars, women are from venus: A practical guide for improving communication and getting what you want in your relationships.* New York: HarperCollins Publishers, Inc.

Kent School District. *Student technology standards in the Kent School District.* Retrieved Nov. 1, 2006, from http://www.kent.k12.wa.us/ksd/it/inst_tech/Standards/student_standards.html

National School Boards Association. (2000). *Plans and policies for technology in education, compendium* (2nd ed.). Arlington, VA: R. Bagby, G. Bailey, D. Bodensteiner, & D. Lumley.

Porter, B. (1999). *Grappling with accountability: Resource tools for organizing and assessing technology for student results.* Sedalia, CO: Education Technology Planners.

Schmoker, M. (1996). *Results: The key to continuous school improvement.* Alexandria, VA: Association for Supervision and Curriculum Development.

Tuckman, B. W. (1965). Developmental sequence in small groups. *Psychological Bulletin* 63, 384-399. Reprinted in *Group Facilitation: A Research and Applications Journal*, No. 3: Spring 2001. Retrieved March 12, 2006, from http://dennislearningcenter.osu.edu/references/GROUP%20DEV%20ARTICLE.doc

Websites

enGauge 21st Century Skills: www.metiri.com/features.html

From Now On—educational technology journal: http://fromnowon.org

Kathy Schrock's Guide for Educators:
    http://school.discovery.com/schrockguide/

National Educational Technology Standards for Administrators (NETS•A)

All school administrators should be prepared to meet the following standards and performance indicators. These standards are a national consensus among educational stakeholders regarding what best indicates effective school leadership for comprehensive and appropriate use of technology in schools.

I. **Leadership and Vision**

Educational leaders inspire a shared vision for comprehensive integration of technology and foster an environment and culture conducive to the realization of that vision. Educational leaders:

A. facilitate the shared development by all stakeholders of a vision for technology use and widely communicate that vision.

B. maintain an inclusive and cohesive process to develop, implement, and monitor a dynamic, long-range, and systemic technology plan to achieve the vision.

C. foster and nurture a culture of responsible risk taking and advocate policies promoting continuous innovation with technology.

D. use data in making leadership decisions.

E. advocate research-based effective practices in use of technology.

F. advocate, on the state and national levels, policies, programs, and funding opportunities that support implementation of the district technology plan.

II. Learning and Teaching

Educational leaders ensure that curricular design, instructional strategies, and learning environments integrate appropriate technologies to maximize learning and teaching. Educational leaders:

A. identify, use, evaluate, and promote appropriate technologies to enhance and support instruction and standards-based curriculum leading to high levels of student achievement.

B. facilitate and support collaborative technology-enriched learning environments conducive to innovation for improved learning.

C. provide for learner-centered environments that use technology to meet the individual and diverse needs of learners.

D. facilitate the use of technologies to support and enhance instructional methods that develop higher-level thinking, decision-making, and problem-solving skills.

E. provide for and ensure that faculty and staff take advantage of quality professional learning opportunities for improved learning and teaching with technology.

III. Productivity and Professional Practice

Educational leaders apply technology to enhance their professional practice and to increase their own productivity and that of others. Educational leaders:

A. model the routine, intentional, and effective use of technology.

B. employ technology for communication and collaboration among colleagues, staff, parents, students, and the larger community.

C. create and participate in learning communities that stimulate, nurture, and support faculty and staff in using technology for improved productivity.

D. engage in sustained, job-related professional learning using technology resources.

E. maintain awareness of emerging technologies and their potential uses in education.

F. use technology to advance organizational improvement.

IV. Support, Management, and Operations

Educational leaders ensure the integration of technology to support productive systems for learning and administration. Educational leaders:

A. develop, implement, and monitor policies and guidelines to ensure compatibility of technologies.

B. implement and use integrated technology-based management and operations systems.

C. allocate financial and human resources to ensure complete and sustained implementation of the technology plan.

D. integrate strategic plans, technology plans, and other improvement plans and policies to align efforts and leverage resources.

E. implement procedures to drive continuous improvements of technology systems and to support technology-replacement cycles.

V. Assessment and Evaluation

Educational leaders use technology to plan and implement comprehensive systems of effective assessment and evaluation. Educational leaders:

A. use multiple methods to assess and evaluate appropriate uses of technology resources for learning, communication, and productivity.

B. use technology to collect and analyze data, interpret results, and communicate findings to improve instructional practice and student learning.

C. assess staff knowledge, skills, and performance in using technology and use results to facilitate quality professional development and to inform personnel decisions.

D. use technology to assess, evaluate, and manage administrative and operational systems.

VI. Social, Legal, and Ethical Issues

Educational leaders understand the social, legal, and ethical issues related to technology and model responsible decision making related to these issues. Educational leaders:

A. ensure equity of access to technology resources that enable and empower all learners and educators.

B. identify, communicate, model, and enforce social, legal, and ethical practices to promote responsible use of technology.

C. promote and enforce privacy, security, and online safety related to the use of technology.

D. promote and enforce environmentally safe and healthy practices in the use of technology.

E. participate in the development of policies that clearly enforce copyright law and assign ownership of intellectual property developed with district resources.

Index

Page numbers followed by f indicate a table.